AF540718

HANDBALL

DPH SPORTS SERIES

HANDBALL

ASHOK KUMAR

DISCOVERY PUBLISHING HOUSE
New Delhi-110002

First Published-1999
Reprinted, 2007

ISBN 81-7141-457-5

Published by:
DISCOVERY PUBLISHING HOUSE
4831/24, Ansari Road, Prahlad Street,
Daryaganj, New Delhi-110 002 (*INDIA*)
Phone: 3279245
Fax: 91-11-3253475

Printed at:
ARORA OFFSET PRESS, Laxmi Nagar, Delhi-92

PREFACE

The need of having a sports series felt because today's situation of the world is not conducive to peace, all round there is destruction, despair, conflict and war; war if not between two nations then within the country itself. In a world where there are some 820 million people unemployed or under-employed, and where 86 million people are born every year, it is not surprising that one out of every four individuals lives in absolute poverty. The *Discovery Publishing House* by Publishing this series seeks to get positive response as—to means by which sports can promote and propagate peace and international cooperation. Sportsmen form a large identifiable cadre. We visualises a situation where a conscious efforts is made all over the world to train the sportspersons to spread the message of peace and international cooperation. Instead of peace keeping efforts through arms and army, the sportspersons may be used as soldiers of peace in a subtle manner. The effort is to make the realize the contribution of sports as a factor for sustainable development, peace keeping and international cooperation.

In developing countries, sports development cooperation is still in the need of justification and steadfast arguments. Many people ask the question "why invest in sports in developing countries for which water supply, health service and agriculture projects are much better suited? An apt reply to this question may be "for many of the people of a developing country, Sports is the only 'Sweaty' Leisure-time activity. Sports represents a moment of joy in the midst of hard poverty-stricken and dirty everyday life. Doing sports even makes one's work go more smoothly the next day.

This series will be useful to the sports promoters, organisers, coaches and other persons related or interested in sports.

Editor

CONTENTS

1

INTRODUCTION

Handball is sometimes called the complete game because nearly every part of the body is exercised. It is a game that can be enjoyed by individual regardless of their age or sex. Although the game is primarily dominated by men, women in recent years are being introduced to it and more and more playing every day. The game of handball may be played by two players (singles), three players (cutthroat) and four players (doubles). It can be played indoors or outdoors on a one-wall, three-wall or four-wall court. The latter, although referred to as a four-wall court is really a five wall game because you can use the two side walls, the front wall the rear wall and ceiling. The four-wall game is also the more complex of the games. It is also the most popular version of the game played. This game is usually played indoors on artificially-lighted, rectangular court while the one-and three-wall versions are generally played outdoors.

The main objective of the handball game is to strike the ball so it hits the front wall in such a way that your opponent will not be able to return it. The game is played until one person or team scores twenty-one points. A match consists of winning two or three games.

Play starts with a serve from any position with in serving zone. The server drops the ball and on the first rebound from the floor strikes the ball so it goes directly to the front wall. After the ball hits the front wall, it may or may not strike one side wall and then bounce on the floor in back of the short line. If the server fails to perform the serve in this manner he loses the serve.

The serve in handball is determined by a toss of a coin in tournament play. During informal play the serve is usually determined by a method called "lagging for the short line.". In "lagging for the short line", each player tosses the ball to the front wall from deep in the court. The player whose rebound from the front wall lands closer to the short line wins the choice of serving or receiving. Since you can only score points while you are serving the choice is very obvious.

After a legal serve puts the ball in play, the receiver must then return the ball to the front wall. On the return to the front wall, the ball may hit any combination of walls—the side walls, ceiling or back wall but not the floor. Once the ball hits the front wall it can only strike or bounce on the floor once before it has to be returned; however the ball may be on the fly or volley.

When the receiver fails to return the ball to the front wall in accordance with the rules, a point is scored for the serving side. As long as the server continues to score points he keeps on serving. If the server fails to return the ball to the front wall, a loss of serve occurs. The play between the serve and the time a point is scored or a loss of serve occurs is called a rally. This is the alternate hitting of the ball by the players or teams. All balls must be hit with the hand. No other part of the body may be utilized.

Values of playing Handball

Handball is becoming increasingly popular with more and more people. The reasons for this are many and varied. The values to be accrued from playing handball are numerous and these values combine to make it an excellent recreational and competitive sport. As schools, YMCA's and athletic clubs make more courts available a greater number of people are experiencing these values. With the televising of national tournaments and special matches and with the construction of courts which provide improved spectator areas handball is being recognized as a sport offering many benefits to the participants.

The game of handball appeals to people of varied age levels and physical capabilities. The man past forty years of age can still enjoy the game for its intensity and duration can easily be controlled. It is not uncommon to see men still playing handball even after they have retired from working men such as Burr supper of Elmira, Robert Dowling of New York, Larry Dike of Tucson and other stalwarts. It is a discouraging thing for the "fireball youngsters" to be soundly trounced by the "clever oldsters" in a lively doubles game. The middle age player can find plenty of competition fellowship and exercise at the handball courts provided by the YMCA's and the athletic clubs. The college age player has many opportunities to learn the game and to compete on campus with a culminating experience in the National Intercollegiate championships. The United States Handball Association has sponsored National Intercollegiate

Tournaments since 1954 and has expanded the program to include divisional tournaments. The National and Regional Junior's tournaments have provided an increased interest in handball for the teenagers. Many fine programs for youngsters are being conducted by various athletic clubs and YMCA's throughout the country. An outstanding example is the program which has been conducted for a number of years by the San Diego YMCA in which the experienced players volunteer to sponsor a neophyte and teach him the fundamental of the game. In handball like so many other sports, the emphasis is an reaching the young people through good instructional programs.

Even though handball appears to be dominated by men the game is not necessarily limited to them as there are many women who enjoy playing handball. In 1951 the first women member joined the Amateur Handball Union and National One-wall Championships for women were first conducted by the United States Handball Association in 1960. Several colleges and universities have had women enroll in handball classes and find them to be good students, especially as the beginners use the larger and softer ball. There is no reason why women should not participate in handball and enjoy it as much as the men do. The skill and desire demonstrated by the fairer sex is equally as knee as that exhibited by the men.

One of the outstanding values of this great recreational sport is the opportunity to experience a vigorous workout in a relatively short period of time and have a good deal of fun while doing it. Handball provides excellent exercise for all parts of the body.

With the proven need for physical fitness this becomes an important consideration. According to many of the studies conducted in relation to physical activity, three games of handball (approximately one to one and one half hours in duration) played three times a week will supply the necessary amount of activity to promote good cardio-vascular health. In addition to the conditioning of the circulatory system the handball player calls into action nearly every must in hits body as he bends, twists lunges and jumps. The handball is hit with either hand and from a variety of positions and angles from overhead to underhand. This overall conditioning of the entire body makes handball an ideal activity when compared to the more popular sports which tend to develop only certain parts of the body. Many collegiate and professional athletes engage in handball during their off-season because they find it to be an excellent way to achieve and maintain a high degree of physical conditioning. There are also many participants representing a variety of occupations who state that playing handball helps them to feel better and enables them to meet the daily demands made of them with greater efficiency.

Another value which many players say is more important to them than the physical rewards is that of a psychological nature. These men state that they go into the court after experiencing tremendous mental strain and nervous tension from the demands their occupation places on them and come out after their match completely exhausted and relaxed. More than one person has said that handball was his tranquilizer. If a person is to stay mentally and physically healthy he must have an outlet for his feelings of aggression and hostility. It is amazing how a few good shots or the chance to smash that little black ball can relieve the psychological pressures which have built up inside a person.

There are no social or racial barriers to the game of handball. The colour of a person's skin has nothing to do with the skill that he has developed. The delivery man can compete against one of the executives of the company he works for. The athlete can compete against his coach. The student can challenge his instructor. The salesman can match his skill against one of his competitors. When two people walk into a handball court there is no allowance made for their race, religion or occupation they are there to play handball. When the game is over they respect each other for their handball skill and competitiveness. New friend ships, and sometimes business contacts, are made in the handball courts.

The "big athlete" has taken over many of our sports today, but not handball. The size and power of a player give him no special advantage in the handball court. The person who has developed the mastery of a variety of shots and the endurance to complete a match without losing his control has the advantage over the power hitter. The small man can play the larger man on equal terms in handball.

A recent survey of college students who regularly engaged in handball revealed that they preferred this activity for the following reasons. (1) There are few rules to learn. When compared to other sports the rules governing handball are quite simple. The basic rules are easy to understand and with the exception of tournament play an official is not required to control the game. (2) There is very little expense involved in the game. This is an important factor for college students. In addition to the usual athletic uniform the only additional equipment required is a pair of gloves and a suitable ball. (3) The fundamental skills can be learned rather quickly (not all players would agree with this idea expressed by the college players). The basic strokes can be introduced in several sessions and then developed to a higher degree of skill as one play. The more advanced skills can be mastered after one has practised and into play the basic strokes. (4) It is easy to arrange a game or to find someone to play with. Handball can be played by two, there or four players so it is not necessary to round up a lot of people to play a game as in softball, football and basketball. Handball players are a friendly group and generally welcome additional players. The popularity of handball in the colleges and universities can be attested to by the demand for more courts and by the excellent courts being constructed and under consideration at many of the schools.

Handball is a game of brains over brawn a truly thinking game, Because of the speed of the game and the way the ball caroms off of the walls, floor and ceiling quick mental reactions are a must. To improve your game you must think in the court as well as play as play in it. Every shot should be carefully studied every mistake carefully analysed. Handball requires and teaches quick mental reactions. This is good training for the immediate decisions needed in everyday life situations.

It would be very difficult to accurately estimate the number of people currently playing handball in the United States. However, one thing is certain and that is the fact that the number of people participating is steadily increasing. This increase in enthusiasts is due to more and more people realizing the values to be gained from playing handball and then actively pursuing these values. Those people who have felt the exhilaration of a fast game of handball have been challenged by this highly competitive sport thereby have become regular participants.

Court play can reduce aggression

Handball players like to mention the release of mental tension brought about by their fast-paced game. Now they have some scientific evidence to back up their claim. That is, if you agree aggression is one of those mental tensions we need to release harmlessly from time to time.

A study by 31-year-old Captain James D. Eaton of the Air Force, assigned to Penn State to earn a master's degree in physical education shows that handball can reduce aggression. And the reduction of aggression doesn't depend on winning. Now teaching at the Air Force Academy, Jim discovered that the out-come of matches played by 32 skilled Penn State handballers was unrelated to aggression changes as measured by a psychology test taken before and after their match.

A scholar with a perfect 40 (A) average in his Penn State course work, Jim plays handball for the recreational and physical fitness benefits. According to his report the research problem he undertook was a test of the hypotheses that handball was an aggression reducer. In the winter of 1971, he administered a standard psychology test called the Adjective Check List to the 24 personality variables measured was analysed.

Before their match, the men had to check off from the list of 300 adjectives those which they felt best described themselves. They took the same test after their match. The difference in the scores measures the rise or fall in aggression.

Of the 32 men ranging in age from 22 to 55 nine recorded a higher score following their match. But their scores weren't nearly enough to overbalance the net loss registered by the other 23.

Such a simple comparison of raw data isn't nearly sophisticated enough to be relied on in this day and age. Statisticians demand "significant: variations in data before any conclusion are drawn and Jim's research is replete with two tailed tests. Wilcoxon matched pairs Mann-Whitney U tests and z-scores. After these calculations were performed the official conclusion was: "The analysis revealed a significant decrease in aggression levels of subjects from the pre-play to the post-play condition."

The won-loss records and the change in test scores were then examined. Tables in the report reveal that 17 players won and 15 lost their matches. (The men didn't necessarily play each other in these non-tournament games).

Of the winners only five apparently couldn't stand prosperity and registered net increases in aggression. The other 12 winners lost aggression points. One lost 21. But there's no accounting for individuality, and one cantankerous guy went up the scale to the turn of 17 points. He also won.

The 15 losers had four among them who chafed under their defeat. According to the scores the aggressive nature of this quartet rose. Again, the statistical searchlights were shown on the winner versus loser data. The result: "There was no significant difference in aggression levels of players from the pre-play to the post-play state when considering the factor of winning or losing a handball match".

The players in this recreational sports didn't worry much about their won-loss record. That's about the way in which many take the game. The player recognize that he's swept a few cobwebs out of his brain and worked some sweat and fat out of his body. These benefits-mental relaxation and physical fitness-recreational sports supposed to offer.

Of the 32 men serving as guinea pigs, five were professional physical educators from the University's College of Health Physical Education and Recreations. The others were amateur jocks and physical fitness buffs from many vocations. Their skill was attested to by tournament standings and the Intramural Office. All were told in a general nature of the reason for the test they took.

A maximum of four players at a time were tested and each flicked through the adjective list swiftly in accordance with the instructions. The test location was the foyer of the "new" eight-court complex built in 1966. Another eight courts, considerably older, are seldom used by Penn State handballers.

Jim's report states that he chose handball for his investigation because "through familiarity with handball and by self observation during play, it seemed apparent that the nature of the game demanded highly aggressive play for a competitor to be successful." Through this natural setting for aggressive play, he left that handball could serve as an attractive medium for the release of that some times troublesome personality quality.

There was another premise a broader one, often articulated by physical educators. "If through continued research it can be determined that physical events can provide an arena for the release and catharsis of aggression then sport has the potential to make a significant contribution to the social well-being of man."

The intent of this work, therefore was to slow what athletics can offer the individual in terms of controlling or releasing his aggressive urges, not what aggression can do for athletics.

The findings of this study tend to support the view that sports help to bleed off mental tension including aggression. But Jim and his advisor, Dr. Dorothy V. Harris associate professor of physical education would hesitate to claim that this study was conclusive proof. To more fully analyse aggression and the relation of the loss of it to physical exercise, they would like to see some research organized around a combination of tests. Also useful would be a comparison of non-physical activities. For example, aggression measurement study of people playing a researchers believe this to be the first aggression changes in people playing bridge should be compared to those evolving from a sports event.

The Penn State researchers believe this to be the first aggression measurement study of people playing a recreational sport. They contrast their work with previous studies aimed at characterizing aggressiveness in athletes fighting for the league title or for a spot in individual standings.

Captain Eaton's report cites the natural sports experience-the joy of competition combined with minimum pressure-as a recreational situation where minimum outside forces come into play. And after all that's what most of us want.

Millions of us who play sports for fun now have some objective evidence to buttress our belief that we receive a mental as well as physical payoff from our recreation.

One thing in common in taking a full study of our stalwart post 40 players....those who continue to perform creditable who enjoy the true competition and reap the "Fountain of Youth" benefits throughout their lives are the ones who keep their weight under control and play the game on a regular basis.

Phil Elbert is no doubt an exception insofar as total physical output at age 41 is concerned. How many fellows around who play the game almost daily then "taper off" in late afternoon with 5-7 miles of sprinting and jogging?

Can a player be at a peak performance after 40? Phil resoundingly gives the answer "yes". He contends after almost 20 years of handball, he is now playing better than ever. *"My control of shots is much better..... stamina-wise with my regime there is no question.... and I honestly feel I can get around the court just as fast as ever before."*

In the past several years Phil has captured six of seven national tiles in the Masters division.... actually six for six in four-wall a second last summer in three-wall.... he has been the road runner counterpart for the outstanding talents singles tournament at Chattanooga in 1972 Phil was able to outlast the field in an exhaustive weekend schedule.

What then would be Phil's chances in the open singles?

"There are too many hard hitters around today for me to really cope with when we talk about national contention. Those bullet serves bother me and if I can't get the ball up to the ceiling or around the walls off the serve, then my opponent has a setup. "In effect this is assertion that there is more first level talent around today than there was a dozen years ago when Phil was a top eight finisher in our open USHA nationals. Instead of just one Hershkowitz, Jacobs Sloan or Oscar Obert of that era, we now find perhaps eight or more of that caliber on the firing line.

We first remember Phil as a novice-type performer in our very first national intercollegiates held at Chicago's Town Club. Phil was an undergraduate at the University of Wisconsin, a defensive back on a Rose Bowl football team and just beginning to get the feel of handball. After a stint in Uncle Sam's forces, Phil was a football coach at Concordia College in suburban Chicago for a couple of years Continuing his handball and winning the USHA central Contenders in 1958 at the age of 26.

His open national championship came with Johnny Sloan at St. Louis in 1964 in the first big tournament held at the 102 acre JCCA. That was Johnny's last big win, although he was only 28 years old. *"When Johnny really was `a hungry' he trained hard," Phil told us. "He did running practised by himself and was really a conditioned athlete, but the desire left him."*

We realize there aren't many players around who will dedicate themselves to Spartan conditioning the way Elbert does. For one thing it takes a good chunk out of the day, secondly, there has to be an almost religious toward dissipation.

Phil does most of his running at a high school football stadium with a perimeter track. In fact, when he was at the national in Austin last March he got shanghaied into a football scrimmage by Darrell Royal's minions.

He will very his running routines and likes to lead up to the grand finale at the end of the summer with a 7 mile stint that includes alternate 100-yard sprints on the gridiron 100-yard runs jog. This follows average speeds of seven-minute miles (4). The 100-yard runs are done at ¾ Speed, and then a jog back, and then a finale-minute mile jog.

We asked Phil if he supplemented his work-outs with any energy pick-ups. *"The only thing I occasionally take is raw sugar."*

We find ourselves categorizing handballers into... (a) conditional players....(b) pure players who play regularly but do nothing to supplement with other type excising.

In recent years Phil has undergone knee surgery and he religiously carried out an exercise program to regain mobility and a return to top tournament play. He did have to compensate for an inability after surgery to twist on his left leg and now utilizes a left first and must face the front wall from short court when using his left.

But, the "road runner" ability is there as attested by his first entrance into the national Masters singles competition. The test at Chattanooga was a rough one, necessitating quarter-finals and semi-finals on Saturday, following a Friday night match. Then on Sunday Elbert met the tough southpaw, Jack Weintraub of New York. In the third game it was Phil's condition that spelled the difference. Jack just couldn't maintain the pace.

Phil keeps himself in streamlined weight control......"I actually eat only one meal a day. For breakfast I'll take orange juice and about five types of vitamin pills... you can hear em rattle around inside of me.....I'll play at the Oak Park Y usually around the noon hour.....and then do my running about 4.30 in the afternoon. My metabolism is no good for early morning running. Along with dinner I may have a few beers, but that's it."

As a bank executive (President of Hillside Trust and Savings) and assorted other business interests Phil has more than his share of pressure and admits, "Handball doesn't actually do the toss-off problem job for me.....I get tense in the competition. It's when I am running that I can forget everything and enjoy the sheer pleasure of getting off by myself and letting off the steam."

And that's the Phil Elbert over-40 handballer. His partner in successfully winning the national Masters doubles Ken Schneider, doesn't carry on nearly as exhaustive a physical program in the over-50 classification. Ken gained national stature as a youngster coming out of New York City and winning the AAU Juniors at the age 18 in New Orleans. He won the open national singles in 1950 at 29 a trio of open doubles with Sam Haber, and Graduated into Masters doubles, winning with Gus Lewis, and now Elbert. Ken has retained amazingly quick reflexes through the years, has through command of both hands and is an all-out competitor. He does not let up on the around like a chess master, and the ability to shoot in the bottom boarders when the shot presents itself. His only weakness, if it could be termed that would then be that of tiring and came on to win back the title.

In the Summer Ken will add weekend golf to his schedule and cut down some of the handball/ racquetball action. During the Fall-Winter season in preparation for the big open nationals he sometimes adds some jogging and more rugged competition against some of the hard-shooting Chicago youngsters in doubles like Don Ardito and Wes Yee. Again, the secret is keeping the weight down....proper rest, enough play to retain the knee edge, and the desire to win.

Of those veterans who remain in serious tournament contention, we find elements in common-no slackening off in the momentum....in other words, no changeover to a different type game such as a pitcher who in losing his fast ball relies on control and "Junk". The "oldsters" in handball may not hit the balls as hard as they once did and may lose a bit of the court coverage, but they still can "muscle" the ball and compensate for the speed loss with better anticipation and knowledge of those four walls.

Moving into the over-60 bracket we have a prime example in Joe Ardito the "kid" who didn't start playing handball until he was 42 at that famed incubator of tournament standouts the Irving Park YMCA in Chicago. Joe now 61 hasn't an ounce of fat on him moves extremely well on the court.....has the natural athlete type of coordination and reflexes and gives that 120% effort at all times. There are no doubts that the streamlined Ardito can maintain the pace at this age because of condition retention of his abilities and of course the experience of many tournaments, covering both open and Masters.

In the introduction of the Super Golden Masters over-60 singles in the second USHA Invitational Masters at Chattanooga Joe had to default in the third game of the finals against another plus-60 marvel, George Brotemarkle, of Los Angeles when he pulled an arm muscle at the onset.

There were 14 entries in that over-60 and they all enjoyed themselves immensely. It brought back some of them to a USHA tournament for the first time in years, and follows the trend of tennis in the older age brackets.

Elbert....Schneider.....Ardito...... and approaching the 70-age mark is USHA president Bob Kendler, who drops everything piled up at his community Builders three times a week to completely toss off pressures at the Evanston YMCA, taking on "all comers" with Joe Ardito in the backfield. Bob couples a "psyching out" technique with a deceptive serve, "educated blocking and scoring and clutch shots when most needed. He more than likes to win as he did in the first two USHA Masters doubles national with Ray Laser back in 1952-53.

2

HISTORICAL BACKGROUND

There is general agreement among sports historians that handball is the oldest of all games played with a ball. It is impossible to place a specific date on the first handball game although some historians believe that it occurred during the early Egyptian era of 4,000 years ago. The writings of Homer tell of the Princess of Corcepa playing "handball" with her maidens and early Aztec drawings reveal young men chasing a small ball as it rebounds from a wall. The Romans found many uses for a ball as described in "Exercises with a small ball" written by Galen in A.D. The Romans played most of the their games in the "thermaeor" baths and one of these games was "pelota" which involved hitting a ball against a wall. It is generally believed that the Romans introduced the game of pelota to the people of the countries they occupied during the Roman Conquests. Variations of this game are still being played in parts of Europe today.

The game of handball as played today originated in Ireland, probably during the tenth century. The game became very popular and was referred to as "fives" representing the five fingers used in hitting the ball. The game played in the early days was slightly different from the game played today. The courts were larger, the ball was harder and travelled faster and the players were allowed to kick the ball as well as hit it with the hands. The people of the Emerald Isle instituted town and country tournaments during the early 1800's and the name that became legend was John Cavanagh of York. The written accounts of his skill leave doubt that he was truly the champion of the day. Following the death of John Cavanagh in 1819 there was no mention of a truly outstanding player until around 1850 when the name of William Baggs became the talk of the handball world. William Baggs is credited with developing the technique of applying spin or "English" to the ball so that it would hop as it rebounded. This style of play added a new dimension to the game and created new interest in handball. For the contributions that he made to the game William Baggs is generally referred to as the father of modern handball. As the Irish immigrants began arriving in the United States so did an interest in handball. Several great handball players came to this country from Ireland in the mid-1800's and among them was Philip Casey. He became instrumental in developing an interest in the game and in the building of handball courts in the eastern part of the country. He was soon classified as the handball champion of the United States and in 1887 was a participant in the first international handball tournament. Philip Casey, representing the United States defeated the Irish champion, John Lawler and thereby became the world champion of handball. Phillip Casey retained this championship for many years and because of his enthusiasm and interest in the sport eventually became known as the father of American handball.

Another memorable name in the history of handball is that of Michael Eagan. He dominated the handball scene for several years following the retirement of Phillip Casey and won the first handball tournament conducted by the Amateur Athletic Union in 1897. The Amateur Athletic Union recognized the potential of this sport and organized a series of tournaments to insure its development as an amateur sport. Around the turn of the twentieth century the game of handball took on a new significance with the addition of "one-wall" handball games and several modifications of the rules. At this time there was a marked shortage of four-wall courts and enthusiasts of the game discovered they could play a game against an unobstructed wall, either indoor or outdoors. The one-wall game originated along the beaches of New York and rapidly gained in popularity for both participants and spectators. The major rule changes concerned the dimensions of the court and the type of ball used. A softer ball was developed primarily to make the game more attractive to beginners as it slowed down the pace of the game and was not so apt to bruise the hands. From this beginning, handball courts of various size and from sprang up all over the United States and today there are one-wall courts, there-wall courts and courts with a front wall and partial side walls in addition to four-wall courts.

The expenses involved in constructing four-wall courts limited the availability of courts for playing four-wall handball. However, its popularity continued to grow and it eventually spread from the East Coast to the West Coast. The YMCA gymnasiums and the local Athletic Clubs contributed to the interest in handball by providing courts and conducting tournaments. The first invitational four-wall tournament was held at the Detroit Athletic Club in 1915, with Fritz Seivered of Angeles in 1919 under the sponsorship of the Amateur Athletic Union. The singles tournament was won by bill Ranft of Lacey, both of Los Angeles. The nation-wide spread of popularity for handball can be seen by reviewing the different cities represented by the winners of the National Singles Championships from 1919 to 1950: Los Angeles St. Paul, Milwaukee, San Francisco, Baltimore Detroit, New York Memphis and Chicago. The four-wall game has become so popular that courts can now be found in many colleges and universities even in some private residences such as the homes of Harold Lloyd of Hollywood and the Vasquez family in West Africa.

The future of handball was greatly enhanced in October of 1951 when the Amateur Handball Union and the Amateur Athletic Union joined forces to establish the United States Handball Association. This organization is considered to be the handball "players Fraternity" and has made great strides in improving the sport of handball. Some of the contributions made by the United States Handball Association include standardized rules, improved equipment teaching clinics, instructional materials multiple tournaments and the use of glass in court construction to provide better viewing for spectators and television and movie cameras. The magazine "Ace" is published bi-monthly by the Association and contains information about players tournaments and special events in addition to instrumental articles. Some of the national tournaments sponsored by the Association are the four-Wall Junior, Four-Wall Championship, Four-wall Womens' Singles, one-Wall Junior, one-wall Championship and the One-Wall Masters. In recent years many of the championship games have been televised both locally and nationally. The United States Handball Association has been largely responsible for the wide popularity afforded handball in the United States.

Handball achieved well deserved recognition as a sport in 1954 when it was granted a niche in the Helms Foundation Hall of Fame in Los Angeles. As one of the first two players selected for the Hall of fame, Joe Platak certainly deserved this recognition. The records established by this man are truly fanatic he won seven national four-wall singles championship in a row, 1935 through 1941, and added two more in 1943 and 1945 after a tour of duty with the United States Navy. He also won in 1938 and 1944. The stories of his many accomplishments in the handball court would fill a book by themselves. George Quam was added to the Helms Handball Hall of Fame, in 1959 and he provided an inspirational theme to the story of handball. He lost his left arm in an accident during his early youth and was told to forget about playing handball. George Quam was not one to give up and he continued to practice until he had mastered the game. In 1930 he was featured in Robert Ripley's "Believe Itor Not" column, at that time he had won twenty four different handball championship titles. President Herbert Hoover invited him to the White House for a personal visit and George Quam is quoted as having commented concerning his handicap, "Your success is not going to be determined by what you have to work with but how you use what you have".

The history of handball indicates that there is a tremendous potential in this sport and as handball reaches new heights the potential increases and the future holds promise for continued growth and success.

3

STRATEGY

A number of handball players have played this game for many years and cannot tell a person what is the basic idea or strategy of good sound handball play, even though they may follow a certain amount of this proper strategy that was learned through years of experience and trial and error. It is important to have a purpose for each shot that you attempt. Granted, there are times when you may be trying your best just to return a tough shot but most of the time will be in a position to choose one of several shot possibilities. Good strategy in handball requires the proper selection of one of three basic shots. Two of these shots are offensive scoring shots and one is primarily a defensive shot.

The *kill shot* is perhaps the most important of the three basic shots and the most difficult to executive. This offensive should be attempted when the ball is at a low position, and you should choose the spot to aim your attempted kill shot so that if it is not a perfect "bottom board" shot, it will be a well-placed shot angled away from your opponent.

The *passing shot* is the second offensive shot and it is just what the name implies. This shot is hit past your opponent and it will effective only if your opponent is in front court (near the short line) or close to one of the side walls. The passing shot must be driven hard, angled close to a side wall, and hit low enough so that it will be most effectively hit from a low position although it is possible to execute this shot from any height.

The volley can be ended by a well executed kill or pass shot. Any other shot that you attempt, your opponent will be able to make the return. Whenever possible, let the ball drop low before contact is made and try to play offensive handball. There will, however, be many times when the ball must be hit from a shoulder-high or higher position. It is very difficult to hit a scoring shot from this height. To attempt to kill shot from this position is foolish because the percentages are against its execution. Your opponent knows this and he will probably drop back a few steps behind the short line and which he is in that position. It will be difficult to pass him. Thus, when attempting a shot from a high position it should be realized that you are on the defense and should attempt at defensive shot. This defensive shot is the third basic shot, the Ceiling shot and it is hit with the idea of moving your opponent to a position close to the back wall from where it is very difficult to hit a scoring shot. The shot serves a second purpose—it gives you time to move up to the all—important front court position.

Good strategy in handball revolves around proper use of these three shots. Each time you attempt a shot use your head as well as the body—choose correctly. Attempt offensive shots when the a ball is low and your opponent is not in good court position-—when the percentages are no your side. When you don't have a good percentage chance of hitting a kill or passing shot, then hit the good defensive shot to move your opponent back to a position where the percentages are against his making a scoring shot.

There is absolutely no particular any thing that a man must have to be an excellent handball player. If you were to say, *"speed Helps", "Shots Help", "Intelligence Helps," "Power Helps,"*—to all of these things of course, "Yes"—but we have seen fine ball players that are fast,—and horribly slow, very tall,—and short—mental giants—and intellectual pigmys.

So what are the real prerequisites to being an excellent ball player? And are the most important of these so-called prerequisites tangible? Can you see them? Can they be measured by comparison of one player cannot be measured by comparison.

Intended to aid

There are a great many terrific handball competitors that are outwardly pathetically ill-equipped with a majority of the above" we have mentioned. But their ability and victories could possibly be measured by *"How much they want to win." "Perseverance,"* and *"A disregard for the probable,"* if such a measuring scale were available.

Let's understand from the beginning that reference to men of the *Hershkowitz* caliber is not intended. Men like that are most assuredly the exceptions and it so such as Vic that people would point if they wanted to take exception to this article. But instructional material is never intended for the Sloans or Collins but rather to the individuals who are looking for a clearcut method to fast improvement. An explanation of *"How much they want to win,"* isn't difficult to define. There are men who want to win so very badly that a their feelings can be the very force that literally gives them the strength they needed in an extremely tough match.

What about "perseverance"? That's the thing that keeps your "fight" channelled in the right direction.—And the only direction you are interested in is the scale of points that go up to 21. You enter the court with that one thought your primary objective is to get 21. Be prepared to ignore a grotesque call by a referee,—you are not fighting him.

Be ready to evaluate the reason behind missing an easy shot.—You are not fighting the ball. It's perseverance that keeps you playing properly,—keeps you thinking properly. It's the thing that creates an obligation in you to yourself not to gratify any impulse that might detour your ability ultimately to win.

Merely fells, it keeps bringing you back to straight thinking no matter what set of circumstances arises on the court.

"A disregard for the probable,"—and a regard for the extraordinary. A man's play is always affected by what he thinks might happen. Handball is a sport that the probable is continuously trampled on.

Out of every one of the these examples there is one thing they have in common. Sooner, or later every handball player runs up against someone he figures to lose to—But there are no probable results only actual results. The cardinal sin then is to let the probable outcome of a match dissuade your efforts to win in any way, physically or mentally. If you figure to lose have a contempt for the probable. There are few experiences in athletics more exhilarating than to a take a conventional outcome and turn it upside down. It's your ticket of a admission to the "Locker Room Liars Association."

So start yourself off in the right direction by trying constantly to win all of your practice games. Associate yourself with winning. We scarcely imagine an association with anything else, in handball, that will give you as much of a push in the right direction. After a while it becomes habit to win a habit that ultimately seems as natural to you as cutting on your gloves.

Handball hints

1. Keep your serve from hitting the back wall when you hop the ball. Your "Landing Area" for hops should be about 6 or 7 feet over the short line at different heights, speeds, and service line positions.
2. Don't Be Stubbron. If you have a pet serve, but a particular opponent is not bothered by it, and is sending you to the rear of the court chasing his return, abandon it and try something else.
3. Learn to make the proper choice when you are on the move. Most good handball players know which choice to make when they are standing still. The very top players can make both choices.
4. Try to be objective as possible when playing and avoid emotional pitfalls. Be repetitious in playing an opponent's weakness.
5. It is rare to see a top player punch (fisting) offensively. Confine your punching to defense.

6. The ceiling shot has revolutionized handball especially the underhand punch to the ceiling with the opposite hand. Don't allow the oldtimers at your club to discourage you from using this shot. Each player has this shot in this arsenal.
7. In a game you only get to hit the ball 50 percent of the time. Learn how to play when it is your opponent's turn to hit the ball. Learn court position. Jacobs and Sloan were masters at this. This two best today are Paul Haber and Stuffy Singer.
8. There are several basic concepts in handball that all of the top players adhere to. Handball is one sport in which it is okay to imitate.

Concentration 'key' to winning Handball

There are some simple tips in the handball that you may be overlooking in your efforts to play a better game. When we say you must concentrate wholly on the play you may replay, "I know all about that," but are you doing it? Believe it or not you have to work at total concentration, it doesn't come easy. In the middle of a hot volley does your mind wander to a high level business meeting you might have later?

In other words forget "all your cares and worries" when you get into the court and enjoy the sheer joys of competition. Sports Illustrated was quoted as saying, *"competition..... is the lifeblood of sport, not victory alone."* Yes, if you buckle down to the task at hand do your best, win or lose you have given it your best shot and the exhilarated feeling of the competition should more than compensate if you happened not to get 21 first.

One of the main weakness of some players is to

get mad at themselves for making an error and by not snapping back and forgetting it they will blow two or three more before righting their ship again. Forget about a misplay or a poorly selected shot that might afford the opponent a setup.

When you get up against a power hitting player you must adjust. You must speed the reflexes shorten your stock somewhat and play deeper court than you normally would do to adjust properly. Again, you can't find yourself returning the ball flatfooted or facing the front wall because you haven't been able to react fast enough. Against the sluggers, unless you can match power with power, you must slow up the pace and throw them off stride. The dynamite slinger likes to work fast....you can change that pace easily by nonchalantly going to return position and taking your time in service....and most important go to the lob service frequently the ceiling around the walls, and try to keep your shots off the back wall for Mr. Bomber.

It is a case of concentrating during the volleys, relaxing immediately after wards. Don't recall the bad games of yesterday or last week, or last month Don't let yourself down. And, whether you're playing No.1 or a bottom-of-the-ladder player play your hardest. Get in the habit of winning concentrated momentum.... and you'll be surprised the number of times 21 comes up!

It would appear almost impossible to maintain real concentration the court without following the ball—*At all times.* Don't stand around flatfooted, turn your back after serving, and then expect to move smoothly to position for volley.

You could have total concentration and completely ignore your opponent. So intent are you on following that ball that you cannot at your foe. Ideally you should "see" your opponent only twice—when you enter the court together and when you shake hands the match is over.

Most everyday, when teaching or being taught the game of handball, tends to emphasize the physical aspect, and rightly so since execution of the various shots is the most important single part of the ol' ball game.

Anybody will tell you that "He's got a great that's why he wins," or "He wasn't in shape that's why he lost," and then there's the world renowned statement, "you got a shoot more".

Well these are all well and good but we all have different physical abilities. Some are strong others not so strong. Some can hit the ball well with their off hands, others can not. Most can bend over but some can't. After the generalities are learned you must set out on your own to find out what type of game suits you best.

What we've like to try and bring out in his article are three of the numerous intangible items, which when everything else is equal, will make the difference between winning and losing and it doesn't matter whether you're a national caliber ball player, or a class double z in your own club. The intangibles make the difference.

You must have heard this word used a least a thousand times every time you have walked into a court. Usually however, it's used in the sentence, "You must concentrate on the ball." If by chance you don't realize the full importance of this statement we suggest you look at some old ACE magazines and notice how the ball players who win the tournaments seem to almost swallow the ball with their eyes. Someone once asked Paul Haber exactly when he watched the ball.

By concentration we don't mean just watch the ball. I mean concentrate on whether to play offence or defence on particular shot. We mean concentrate on getting into position early enough so as not to be forced to hit the ball while you are on the run. Concentrate on hitting the ball, at all times to an area which is predicated not on where the ball is, but where your opponent is. In other words try and have some basis of thought some reason for doing whatever it is you are doing.

This one's a little tougher to master because success is what breeds confidence.

You must have confidence in your ability to make correct decisions. Confidence that you can make your particular repertoire of shots. Confidence that you can win the game. Unfortunately, its easier said than done.

One of the ways we used to develop confidence in my shots was to go into a court by myself and practice hitting certain shots. The theory behind this was that during an hour's practice session we would probably get to hit hundreds of the same shots over and over again until such time as we could make them consistently. This is very unlike game conditions where if you get 10 to 20 chances to make the same shot during the course of a match it is a lot. The concentrated practice also serves another purpose.

Since during a game you are penalized by means of points if you miss, the result is usually a slight loss of confidence. Conversely, the mind during practice seems to reject the errors and record only the successful attempts.

As far as confidence in your ability to win games, I think the words of Vince Lombardi pretty well sums it up. "Winning is a habit." There's only one way to acquire this habit and that's to Win. No matter how many points you allow your opponent and whether it's practice or a tournament you must win every game possible. If you do this pretty soon you start to get the feeling even though it's never true you think it's true and that is what's important! So believing this you should go right out and pick an argument with your wife, and win it—by all means win it.

This last one is the toughest because a lot of intangibles wrapped up in one. We think you might as well call it the courage of your convictions. The best way that we can explain it is to relate to you my feelings regarding percentages. We feel that there is always a high and a wrong thing to do with all shots. We do not feel that the circumstances change the percentages. It is may opinion that if a shot is the correct one to take at 0-0 in the first game, that it's the correct one to take at 20-20 in the third.

A couple of years ago Stuffy Singer wrote a very interesting article for ACE entitled "The three C's of Handball" in which he discussed Concentration Courage and Confidence.

To quote: "a man who uses his hand only is called a labourer, and a man who uses his head only is called an apprentice but a man who uses his hand, head, and heart is an artist." It is these H's-Hand Head and Heart that we want to discuss.

1. *Hand:* This refers to shot execution being able to hit ball where you want to. The mastery of the various serves and the several offensive and defensive shots obviously essential to any player. Hitting a particular shot is a specific motor skill that can learned by repetition. You can learn to hit the ball anywhere you want to with either hand if you are willing to work enough. If there is a secret to the mastery of any particular shot it is concentrated practice. The proper execution of just one new shot can really improve your game. Often a player will go into the court to work on improving his game, and he will hit 15 or 20 back wall 1 shots and a similar number if kill shots, pass shots accuracy that you already possess, but there must be much more emphasis on a particular shot if you are really looking for improvement. What we suggest is that you should decide to learn one new shot and then go on into the court and hit that shot until you learn it. It might mean hitting the same 200 times a day for a month. You might ask "Does anybody ever spend that much time just practising one shot?
2. *Head:* This refers to shot choice-choosing the correct shot to hit according to the situation. The "Situation" can involve quite a number of things. What is your sequence of thoughts as you are lining up a shot? In discussing this subject with some of our leading players, most of them out their thoughts into this order: (1) What is my opponent's position in the court? (2) Where is my position?

(3) What is the height of the ball when I hit my shot? (4) What are the best shots to attempt according to the answers of the first three questions? (5) Which of these shots can we execute and which of these are my best "percentage" shots? (Right here it might become evident as a shot you don't know how to hit that would be useful to your game-learn it!) (6) What shot did we attempt last time in this same situation? Also very important in shot choice is your opponent you play is different and you should have a weakness? Every opponent you play is different and you should have a game plan for each one, designed to take advantage of your strength and his weakness. This involves analysing not only his style of game but also things such as his speed and endurance. Are you going to try to wear him down with pass shots and ceiling shots? May be if his name is Pete Tyson won't change your game plan if it is not working. You have nothing further to lose by changing and you might find the answer to his game.

Will just thinking really mean that mush to your game? Talk to some young strong player who has just been beach badly by a man at least 30 years older. The younger player was stronger faster, had better stamina, hit the ball harder, and may even have had better shot execution. So why did he lose? Use your head.

3. *Heart*: The third "H" is heart. This is the intangible. What does it mean? It's been called several other names such as desire drive the will to win. You see it in the player who fights you tooth and toenail for every point-also in players who never give up no

matter what the odds. You hate to run up against one of these players in a tournament because you know you've really got a fight on your hands. He can never be taken lightly even if he doesn't have the skill that you do. He doesn't understand the word "quit". He is the creator of "upsets". He's the player who gets the most out of his ability. Someone once said that your performance in any sport about 20% ability and 80% what you do with that ability. You rarely see a national or world champion who doesn't possess this ingredient we call "heart". But also see it in players who don't have the physical ability of the best, but nevertheless occasionally rise up to the super status physical of their overwhelming desire.

Let's deliver into some of the aspects of playing our game:

Flexibility: As Stuffy Singer puts it simply; it is obvious some players are able to bend better, get power for their shots and thus shoot with more authority. Dr. Steve August is an excellent example of this ability to get low and with his long reach he gets ideal contact and bombing velocity on his shots. At 6'2", Steve with this asset can also have the advantage on high shots making the ceiling shots less effective against him, plus using his long reach.

Is there anything a player can do to increase this bending ability? Yes, we would prescribe stretching exercises....skipping rope for more quickness... situps.....one good exercise is to cross the legs then bend over and touch the left foot with the right and the right foot with the left hand alternately.

Many players find it difficult to get going in a first game.... much of this is caused by not warming up long enough or doing some of the things necessary to prepare for the quick stop and start movements and the need to get low for shots.

You just can go into the court throw a few balls around and expect to jump into the action at full efficiency. It is helpful to do stretching exercises while in the locker room.... then follow up in the court with some more before even touching the ball. If there is a jogging track or gymnasium or even a treadmill you can aid in your warmup. In other words get the "juices" Flowing. Start slowly after the exercise with loosening up movements overhand and sidearm with the ball....practice shots from various positions on the court and with both hands, then move into the overhead shots high around the walls and to the ceiling.

Don't give yourself a handicap of a slow first game start by now being prepared.

Momentum is most important in winning handball and to allow your opponent the lead can give him both that advantage and the mental confidence that means so much.

Be ready to go from the gun!

When Wes Yee jumped off to an 11-0 lead on Paul Haber in their first game of the recent national 3-wall at Columbus it was evident that Paul was not loosened up properly and he confirmed this after the match. Usually he will give his warmups adequate attention stroking the ball with good authority and practising all the shots.

There are too many matches lost by players who try and pace themselves. In singles there can be letdowns....It is too difficult to regain stride after "easing up". It's those "amazing gets and shots" that spell the difference.

Don't give up during the volley against a strong defensive shot which you feel even if returned will provide a setup. No. 1—You dishearten an opponent by being able to return his best shot.... No. 2.—Even if you return it weakly he may "blow" the setup through an over-eagerness to bottom board it, or hurry his shot because he is discouraged that you could get the ball back.

How many times have you seen a player "break his neck" to return a seemingly sure pass from deep court with his opponent in front court ready to pounce on the next shot and then ingloriously either floor it or hit it too hard and it comes up enough for you to get back into the volley?

The difference in letting the pass go to conserve petrol and in straining hard to return it can mean more than a handout or point it can readily lead to a few more points....this is the changeover in momentum and desire.

A Gordie Pfeifer is feared by his opponents because he never gives up. Sure, he may lose a tough three-game match now and then because he puts so much of himself into the battle that he'll end up with leg cramps but those same tactics of all out handball have won two national invitational single's crowns. Gordie will return a ball from a scrambling prone position if he can.

Terry, Muck, our current national singles champ is another who feels it necessary to go "for broke" during the volley;" "I try to run a mile a day before playing in practice sessions," Terry told us, "and then we get used to playing hard while getting tried as happens in tournament conditions. When asked about the theory of going for everything he was inclined to opine, "Retrieving is a big part of my winning or losing and if we can pick up my opponent's best short the next time he shoots he will try and make it finer and may lead to an error. You never know what will happen if you can pick up a shot so my game is to go for 'em all."

Paul Haber had made mention of the many little things that go into the championship play. He has learned to study his opponents know by their body action what they will do with the ball and thus get that very valuable jump on the ball. "It's knowing what to do with the ball when you are behind your opponent that's so important.....whether to go left or right. In three-wall I must keep a driving volley going to set up the shot.....in four-wall it's the controlled ceiling shot that can do the volley job for me to a great extent.

Paul adds, "Too many of the younger players refuse to listen to us. They think they know all the answers. One will say, "My serve is working great".....another will tell me, "I'm really hopping the ball and getting power. But these fellows don't think enough in the shots will spell victory every time. There's a lot of tournament players who can out-power me, hit the ball both ways, volley with both hands real well, but when it gets down to the nitty gritty they can't put their game together, Why? C-O-N-T-R-O-L. The serve is certainly a big part of the handball arsenal. Again it's the control of that serve that is most important. When Dr. Steve August is hot with his serve he's going to get a half dozen aces or more a game and that's huge handicap to overcome. Again a Haber feels he cannot run the jeopardy of a sore arm trying to power any kind of a hop and is content in the main to get a defensive return rather than an unplayable ace. He is so sure of his volleying game that he can afford to overlook the plus factors of point serves.

Vic Hershkowitz had the most effective serve we have ever seen but throwing all those hops led to arm trouble. Jim Jacobs had a tremendous serve also with two way hops and also threw a lot of "stuff" on the ball off deep side wall and back wall shots. He, too would suffer tightness in the arm that would keep him from throwing those hops at crucial times in tournaments.

The Haber answer to overcoming the big server is to limit his number of serves, and that isn't an easy solution. The concentration on big innings and total determination to set up the proper shot and not get reckless when on the receiving end is his ultimate game plan.

There's complete flexibility to the number and types of serves, changes of position in the serving area, using low, power driving serves....getting the ball chest or shoulder high to the offhand which is usually the vulnerable area of most opponents.....this can be done with simple half speed side arm into the back wall corner....the cross-court serve....always with the opportunity of varying speeds....the serves to the strong hand, mixing them up. Although it may be natural hand, many players have trouble in lateral movements that way.

Keeping the ball off the back wall is a main problem with the so-called "Club" player; pounding the ball off the serve or in volley and giving the opponent is setup off the back wall. The only thing to do when such a shot is presented your foe is to move quickly toward that front wall as he shoots with the possibility of picking up that shot and then having him a sitting duck in deep court.

There was a practice routine used at the Los Angeles Athletic Club a decade or more when Jim Jacobs represented that Club and Danny Phillips was the handball commissioner. Danny was a film buff and produced one instructional film, "Never hit the Front Wall First"...neophyte players were taken in the court and told to volley the ball but to keep the ball from hitting the front wall first. If they violated this axiom they lost the serve or point.

This is good practice but not altogether reasonable as there are many opportunities off the serve or volley to go front first....position of the opponent during volley....type of serve that can be pinpointed to the front wall low and driving down either wall.

Players don't take advantage of the four walls and ceiling. "Ring Around the Rosy" is a term used in bringing the ball around the walls high with a two fold purpose....to bring opponent into deep court and not allowing him to position himself solidly for the return, and the same time allowing yourself to get that commanding short line-center position. Again using the Haber Example as he can serve superbly as a model on handball tactics and theory, we have seen Paul play opponents with the agreement not to use the ceiling at all and then drive them crazy with his round-the-walls control which can well be as effective as the controlled ceiling shots.

There's also the hard, around the walls shot line position or even closer, in that will die off the side wall in deep court and is most difficult to return.

In total summation, it's control you want to attain in your game. Rather than try and use the whole range of serves and shots just concentrate on those shots. And then you'll be amazed on how much easier it will be to reach that magic number—21!

Would you advise the average player after using a ceiling shot from deep court to move up to center position on the shot line? We know you are to hang back most of the time but have the quickness to move up in time if necessary'.

— First you have to decide after shooting the ceiling ball is whether the ball will go to the back wall or not. If you see your opponent is going to take the ball off the back wall then we would run in to the short line or a little further. Chances are the average player will a attempt to kill the ball or will hit it in low because he can't get the proper leverage for anything else. If the ceiling shot is good to drop in deep court then we would stay in deep court.

When you play a Jacobs or a yambrick and shoot a ceiling shot what is there usual return?

— If we hit a ceiling ball to Jim on the left side we'll stay deep because he won't shoot with his left hand off this shot whether it comes off the back wall or in deep court. He will hit a two or three wall return or a attempt a pass down the right. Yambrick has ability to kill with his left hand off the back wall and very effectively but his ball always hooks to the right and if it comes up it will come off the side wall and we can stay back as we have the time to get into position with the ball hanging. He shoots often if the ball comes off the back wall far enough.

Importance of serve. Paul, you don't necessarily count a lot of aces off your serve. What do you try and do though?

— We try to force return from our opponent's off hand on the serve. Assuming most of the opponents are righthanded we serve to the left with a reverse and we try to keep from going to the back wall. In other words we want our opponent to hit the ball underhand with his left hand and hopefully he'll get in to a ceiling volley with me.

Now very few players in the use "stuff" on the ball with the serve or during the volley. Do you think it's possible for the club a player to learn how to hop the serve?

— To learn how to hop the serve effectively is very helpful to a game but we don't recommend that this player work on it. We think this should be the last step to learn after the rest of the game has been perfected. A hook takes a lot out of the arm and a lot of control to be effective. Many players hook the ball but it costs them points. You'll notice that most of the players who hook the ball a lot lose a lot of speed from their arms in the second game of a tough match. One of the hardest hitters—Oscar Obert—hits very hard ball but so strong throughout a grueling tournament. We think if Oscar did employ a big hook his arm would tire in late stages of key games.

With the amount of handball Oscar has played—one wall three-wall and four-wall it is most likely he would have suffered a lot of arm trouble with use of hooks.

How about the cross court serve?

— The cross court serve is good but to a lot of players it is hard on their arms because of the motion they use. In the nationals we can't start off mentally to go at a burst of speed not because it will wear me out physically. Our outlook is usually very blase. The fighting spirit doesn't seem to be there and builds up in the later rounds, we don't believe that any good player can be high for the first couple of days of the tournament and maintain that level all week. We do get a chance to sharpen up this way.

One of the problems we have in high level tournaments is the capabilities of referees. We have talked about the possibility of an association but just to certify referees won't solve the immediate problems. What we probably need are a lot of clinics and point out to potential referees what they should do when they referees match. We have always preached taking charge. What do your suggest Paul as a possible solution to our problem?

— During the last year in the various clinics we have conducted across the country the question always comes up about refereeing. We try to explain to the fellows that a referee must have 100 percent control of the game and shouldn't be abused by the crowed in any fashion and he shouldn't be aware of what the crowed says as regards any calls. However, referees are subdued by the crowed and some of the players. We also believe that a referee should contrary to what is being done should make their calls must faster on the hinders and slower on the short calls.

It is very disconcerting to a player to have the referee call a short the ball goes six or seven inches over the line. Most referees call the short immediately on the bounce and we consider this premature. The receiving player is going to swing at the ball and a slower call won't affect the play.

On hinders—we don't know whether we should go into avoidable hinders at this stage-but they are happening all the time all over the country and there's possibly only three referees who will make the call possibly because they think they'll lose a friend. Well we don't feel that way. Its got to be called one way or the other.

You use a very effective left hand kill into right wall front wall from position near or in front of short line.

— We started using this shot about two years ago. We developed it as an alternate to the ceiling. We usually don't attempt to shoot it more than two or three feet beyond the service line. It's not effective from deep court. Because more balls come to my left doubles than in singles we naturally use it more playing doubles.

Do you put anything on this shot?

— A very slight natural hook never a reserve spin on it. Once it this the side wall, coming from the left side with my left hand it loses a lot of its speed and as a result dies out a lot faster than a left side wall-front wall kill with the left hand. It takes quite a while to develop this shot to get the knack of getting the control so that the ball isn't floored too much.

We haven't seen anyone use this shot open-handed except by a accident. Johnny Sloan will use this shot effectively with his first. Lance Zepp, I remember used this shot with his right hand into the left side wall-front wall very good.

Speaking of various sized courts along the tournament exhibition trail. For example the Dallas A.C. where you have had some thrilling matches with buzz shumate who practically owns that court. How do you compensate for your game in this kind of court? What changes do you make?

— In a small court and in that 18+36 Dallas A.C. court with the 20-foot ceiling, we have to practically abandon the ceiling game unless we can hit one certain ceiling shot that runs into the side wall off the ceiling with either hand from either side This is only way to make the ball slow down and not jump off the back wall. If the ball is hit to the ceiling on this court there is no way to make the ball die out in deep court as can be done on the 20+40 court. The court is just too short.

Like most handballers we prefer singles play. A singles match provides a good work-out in a short of time. It gives us more opportunities to hit the ball. It offers us a chance to sharpen our game when a better player has to play us because we reserved the court before he did. In recent years however doubles play has become very popular. This is partially because it has become more difficult to reserve a court for singles. The construction of new courts has not kept pace with the popularity of the game; never mind the ever growing popularity of racquetball. A random visit to almost any court at any "y" athletic club or military installation—particularly during those prime times of 11 a.m to 1 p.m., and 4.30 p.m. to 9.30 p.m.,—will show that necessity has dictated doubles matches as the order of the day. But doubles play is also popular, because it presents the challenge of teamwork and does not tire out as easily as singles. Players of about equal ability have found it to be an exciting and enjoyable game.

Since this is true, more double instructional material should be made available at the grass roots. Haber's *Inside Handball* has a short and useful section about doubles play. *Handball magazine* contains occasional bits and pieces of doubles instruction here and there, and *handball illustrated* contain a few tips.

But there should be more doubles instruction published and it should somehow get to those who need it, perhaps by somewhere in the locker rooms or near the entrance to the courts. As it is many doubles teams even though they consist of good individual players, never know the satisfaction of playing as well as they could.

Ruby Obert, who holds 35 national doubles titles (He and his brothers Oscar and Carl, hold 90 national titles) believes that teamwork is the most crucial factor in doubles play and that partners must play together regularly to achieve proficiency as a team. This of course is obvious," he said in a recent interview, " but partners must also know how to play as steam. Unlike football and basketball there are no set partners or formations that will guarantee successful teamwork. The game moves too fast. Besides if the opposition catches your team in a pattern it will exploit it.

Obert chooses to talk about achieving teamwork in terms of a game plan. "Part of this plan is deciding who will dominate the play and who will play a supporting role". He said. "Assuming both players are righthanders the player on the left is usually the one who dominates. He covers center court with his strong hand. He controls the pace of the game. He is the shot-maker. His job is to keep his team on the offensive and score. Needless to say he is the strongest player.

On the other hand the supporting player on the right "Seldom attempts a kill shot and only when it is a hanger," Obert said. "His task is to keep the ball moving and the opposition on the defensive. He attempts to set his partner up for the decisive shot".

Many handballers do not like to play the supporting role. They think that it is too easy to play and does not offer enough of a challenge. Others feel that it does not permit them to get much of a work-out or to hit ball enough. If one's goal is merely to get a good work-out or to hit the ball often, there is some merit to the latter objection. As for the first objection experienced doubles players know that the supporting role is both difficult and challenging. It requires self-discipline to retrain from taking shots that belong to one's partner good judgment to select the right shot from among several that could be taken the skill to execute each shot properly—keeping in mind that the objective is to keep the opposition on the defensive and to set one's partner up for the decisive shot. Moreover, "Many experienced doubles players agree that the supporting player gets the "junk" Obert said, "and yet is expected to be consistent. Consistency in returning junk is not easy. This is where the real challenge lies."

Ruby, who usually plays the supporting role, is the ideal expression of this self-discipline good judgment skill and consistency. He never takes a shot that belongs to his partner. He supports his partner with a variety of shots designed to keep the opposing team on the defensive straight shots or ceiling shots down the right side close to the wall; high "Z" shots from the front wall-left side wall in to the deep right coming off the side wall; and passing shots or ceiling shots down the left side wall. He always attempts to set up his partner for the decisive shot. Occasionally however, when he has the opportunity to fly kill or kill he takes it.

Another part of the game plan "is to decide who will take what shots and to help each other with voice signals," Obert said who will take the shots that angle off the side walls? Will each partner play all balls front and back court that are on his side? What voice signals should be used? Partners who play together regularly usually know the answers to these questions so that each of them can play with single-mined abandon. "Partners who do not decide on these matters or do not stick to their decision usually cross up one another at least a few times a game and a few points is often the difference between winning and losing.

He considers voice signals important not only when there is doubt as to who will play a particular shot but also when one's partner is backing up to play a ceiling shot rebounding close to the back wall. "It is important to tell your partner—quickly—how to play that shot off. the back wall or before it hits the back wall" he said. "You are in a better position to judge what shot he should take". In a recent two-game match ruby helped his partner several times on that particular shot and made the right call every time.

A key factor in any game plan is to ascertain the weaknesses of the opposition and exploit them relentlessly. "Blessed are the merciful" was not meant for the handball court. If one opponent is a weaker player than this partner, it would be foolish to play his partner. If the opposing team is made up of right-handers one weakness is usually the offhand of the player on the left side. "He should be forced to take many shots with his left hand both serves and volleys," Obert said. "Early in the match he may make strong returns of these shots but his arm will eventually tire. Causing him to make weak returns or errors." If the opposing team consists of a righthander and a lefthander the middle of the court is wide open to exploit with front wall-side wall shots low fast shots down the middle and the hook serves and volleys which fade away from the player on the right and into his partner's body." In addition to studying your opponent's weakness you should watch for obvious errors and weaknesses in your team's play and attempt to correct them.

Ruby also stresses the importance of the serve in every game plan. The ideal serve, of course is an ace or one that forces weak return and every player should attempt the ideal serve. "Typically, this serve either catches part of the or more walls before or after it this the floor of the back court," he said. "The side wall or a Z serve. The player on the right serves to hit the short line and back wall or a left or right hop over the short line to the left side."

Generally, weak returns "should be quickly killed by the left court man, usually for a right wall-front wall kill," Obert said. "This kill shot is the best one to take especially in doubles, because it moves away from the opposing team, where as the wall-front wall shot moves towards the opposition and is easier to return. "Sometime, however, the opposition to return this shot and "the partner who returns the ball should attempt a driving pass shot that hits the side wall near mid-court but does not each the back wall. This wall keep the opposition off-balance hopefully result in a score.

Your opponents will also be attempting to score aces and to force weak returns with their serves. They will try to move you off-balance and out-of-position with their serves and volleys. "Therefore it is good to remember that you can return serves and volleys to the ceiling and around the wall," Ruby said "Generally either of these returns will buy time to get your team back into position."

Finally Obert said, "avoid playing in a pattern. Mix up your shots and change the rhythm of the game. Keep the opposition off-balance in the same way that a baseball pitcher does when he mixes his pitches." Many doubles teams know this every time attempt the same shot too frequently or consistently leave the right front corner unguarded. "An alert opposition will exploit any pattern by anticipating shots moving into position and making a strong return. If a player notices that his partner or team is playing in particular pattern, he should call a time out and talk it over. Do not hesitate to change a losing game."

"Teamwork—knowing how to play as a team, helping one another and playing together regularly, that is what doubles play is all about," Obert said. "No matter what the score, keep playing for many a cause has been turned into a victory. Also, always cheer your partner and encourage him, even if he misses, a few."

Being in good physical shape is a must for any top-class handball player, or anybody for that matter. There are several exercises which will get an individual in good shape, but for the handballer there are four which we strongly recommend: (1) Push Ups, (3) Sit Ups, (3) Skipping Rope, (4) Short Sprints.

Physical fitness surveys indicate that, on average, a man reaches his peak of physical fitness, speed and stamina, in the age range of 23 to 26. Of course it is the rate of the down trend that is the all-important factor. The rate of physical determination from 28 onwards will be gradual, moderate or fast depending upon the natural physical endowment of an individual and the consistency of his efforts to maintain fitness.

Handball is definitely a running man's game and this where the physical conditions of the individual has a bearing.

The Push Up: does it do for the handballer? It builds strength in the upper arms adds muscle strength and endurance to the biceps and the deltoid muscles which are the muscles at the point of the shoulder that often creates painful problems for the handballer. It also develops and tones the breast muscles. From 10 to 30 repetitions.

The Sit Up: Lie back knees flexed, heels on the floor, hands clasped behind the neck or extended backwards. Have someone hold your feet down if necessary. Roll up slowly to a sitting position. Roll back slowly and repeat making sure you are exhaling on the upward movement and inhaling on the backward movement.

Correct breathing is important for this exercise as it also helps beneficial. It creates the habit of saying on the balls of your feet, while at the same time strengthening the leg and thigh muscles which are very important for the playing of handball.

Short Sprints: 5 to 10 yds. over a 100 yd. stretch. Again it helps develop the habit of stopping and starting which is so much a part of the handball game.

Deep breathing is also a must-as you strike the ball you should be exhaling. It is very important to take in plenty of air after a tough rally. The Oxygen snaps you back quickly.

The mental approach

When you find out who your opponent is going to be you should start your game plan. Calculate your opponent's capabilities. Ask yourself is he a little over-weight that will slow him down, or is he a born miler. Does he warm up slowly? If this is so your game plan might include short rallies and quick kills and easy shots in the corners to score a lot of points before he warms up.

Suppose your opponents off-hand appears to be especially weak. Resolve then to hit the ball to that weakness, whenever possible. Or say he is not good off the back wall give him plenty of shots in this area.

Of course your opponent will be sizing you up at

the same time., and have formulated a game plan also. Perhaps he might think you are short winded and he might be planning to hit the ball away from you to keep you running for the first game. If you spot his game plan, make sure and alter your plan, race in and take the ball on the fly, giving him little time to get set to run you.

There is rhythm and tempo to victory and defeat. In hurling one team is behind gets hot and ties the game. The same happens in handball and when it does something has to be done, otherwise you will up a loser. Slow down the tempo, break your opponents concentration. Use the "shoe excuse", open and close the lace, making believe it's hurting you.

In the U.S. players are allowed time outs. Most players advise against trying to retrieve the seemingly impossible- and so do for the most part, If we think it is really impossible. The theory is that trying for the seemingly impossible retrieves takes too much out of you. We have found that by returning some of these seemingly impossible retrieves and ultimately winning the rally, psychologically we have won a great deal more than the point or serve. We like to imagine our opponent thinking "Here we pound in our best shot and he digs it up: How will we beat him?

Handball is a "psyche" sport and you have to get it working for you. Against some opponents a bit of bragging before the game works-e.g. We have been training hard for the past three weeks. Against other players the opposite works.

After a match is over, win or lose look back on it, make mental notes as to what you could have done that would improve your performance. Play and practice yourself through the kind of situations you encountered in a losing game.

Beneath the championship level are many, levels of competition with small trophies but big memories—and just plain old handball. Whether you play for fun, conditioning or trophies your skills and enjoyment will increase if you play as if there is no substitute for winning.

4

CONDITIONING

Suggested warm-up exercises for Handball players

Prior to participating in the strenuous handball match, it is recommended that you warm up your muscles properly. Many research studies have indicated that athletic performance is enhanced by a proper loosening up period. A proper warm-up that increases your flexibility and stretches the muscles to their maximal length will help to prevent injury and add more power to your shots.

The pre-game warm-up is even ore important to the "week-end warrior" and those players in the seniors, masters and golden masters divisions. The maintenance of flexibility helps to prevent many of the aches and pains that are common with advancing age.

Very few, if any, handball players would consider playing a match without warming-up. Although the need for the values of loosening the muscles up have been common knowledge for many years, what is not common knowledge was the proper method of obtaining maximum flexibility.

Maximal or optimal flexibility can be achieved safely by utilizing a well-rounded program of static stretching exercises. This method is preferred over the ballistic or bounching method because the latter expends too much energy and is likely to cause post game soreness. There is also the danger of overstretching or exceeding the extensible elastic limits of the muscle or tendon group in question while performing this type of movement. On the other hand, static stretching exercises permits the connective tissue and the muscle being exercised to be elongated safely because of the slow and steady stretching that takes place.

The following are static stretching exercises that are recommended as a pre-game warm-up to participating in a vigorous handball game or match. After completing these exercises, you should then move into the final phase of the pre-game warm-up. This last phase consists of throwing and hitting the ball easily at first and then slowly increasing the tempo utilizing or performing the different types of shots executed during a game.

STATIC STRETCHING EXERCISES

1. *Gastrocnemius (Calf) Stretcher:* Start this exercise with your body in an erect position with your feet about one or two feet from a wall. Next place your hands on the wall approximately chest high. Keeping the heels of your feet on the floor bend the elbows of your arms until your head touches the wall. Repeat several times increasing the distance of your of your feet from the wall.

2. *Hamstring stretch:* To start this exercise, you should take a sitting position on the floor with your legs extended and the toes pointing toward your head. Then lean forward placing your hands on your

shins. Repeat this exercise several times, each time moving your wrists closer to your toes.

3. *Upper Trunk Stretcher:* Start this exercise by lying in the prone position. Then, place your hands several inches in front of your shoulders with the palms of your hands in contact with the floor. Next while keeping your pelvis on the floor, extend your arms so that your chest is raised from the floor. Exhale, then repeat this exercise several times moving your hands closer to your shoulders with each effort.

4. *Trunk Twister:* Start this exercise with your body in an erect position. Without moving your feet, turn your upper trunk to the left. For leverage, place your right hand on your left hip and your left hand behind your back on your right hip. Exhale, repeat twisting motion several times and then reverse the direction of the twist.

5. *Shoulder Girdle:* To start this exercise, stand erect with your hands at your sides. Shrug your shoulders as high as possible and pull them back as far as possible. Continue to pull your shoulders down and back to the starting position. Repeat this exercise several times and reverse the direction of motion.

6. *Shoulder Joint:* To start this exercise, you should stand erect. Then bring your right hand up and over your shoulder on your right side to the upper part of your back. Next place your left hand behind your back and try to clasp your fingers together. Repeat this exercise several times and then reverse it by bringing the left arm over your left shoulder and your right hand behind your back trying to clasp your fingers on the opposite side.

Interval training: advantages for Handballers

"Interval Training—work or exercise followed by a properly prescribed relief (rest) interval- is superior to continuous exercise training programs." With this opening sentence authors Edward Fox and Donald Mathews plunge into a unique means of training for any sport-from ping pong to football (To handball). In their recently book, Interval Training: Conditioning for Sports and General Fitness, these two physical education buffs define interval training, dwell briefly upon the physiological and biochemical reactions involved in exercise and set up numerous example interval training programs for a variety of sports.

If one is not immediately compelled to rush out and part with $5.95 for 275 sweat spawned pages of college oriented physical education literature, perhaps a review of this book's main principles, programs and especially the relationship of these principles and programs to racquetball might suffice. The work is divided into three portions, which will be expanded upon below.

The main concept behind *Interval Training* is alluded to above in the initial sentence of this article, and it is worth rereading right now. Stated in other words, if one were to utilize running to get in shape for handball, a superior work-out would include exercise punctuated by rest periods rather than continuous running. Thus we have a simplified definition for Interval Training: It is non-continuous exercise.

Pioneered by track and swimming coaches, Interval Training is the superior way to condition the body. It requires less time to perform and provides more rapid progress than any other training technique, according to the authors. The gut reaction to this last statement is probably, "I always thought that the longer and harder I worked the more conditioning benefits I'd reap. To dispell this popular belief a short summary of the book's part one, "Physiological Considerations", is presented. These less scientifically oriented and just not at all interested in an in depth study of something like, Glucose plus 02 plus Stress-ATP plus Lactic Acid, may skip on the next portion of the book, part two, "The Interval Training System." In this section specific condition programs for shaping up for sports (handball included) will be presented. In part three, "Special Considerations," a hodge-podge of helpful hints relating to physical exertion are given.

Einstein gone wild

As Fox and Mathews outline in part one, a complex series of chemical reactions occur when a body performs a physical activity. An Einstein type might experience mild exhileration upon persuing these equations. However, in such matters most people appreciate the outcome rather than the rational. Therefore, this review need only be concerned with the end product of these puzzling chemical reaction (adenosine trip phosphate ATP). If ATP does not sound that profound, it should. Basically it is the energy reserve in a muscle; any muscle. There are two ways in which ATP may be supplied to the muscle cells. The first of these methods is called Anaerobic because oxygen is not a prime ingredient on the ATP product. The second method is termed Aerobic because oxygen is a prerequisite for ATP syntheses. How does one distinguish which of the two energy systems is utilized during certain exercises? The source of ATP will depend upon how long it takes to perform the physical task. For example, the 100-yard dash and the two mile events each require a predominately different ATP energy system. Thereby one does not train for the two mile run (oxygen system) by running 100-yard dashes (Anaerobic Systems) in practice.

Handball depends almost entirely on the Anaerobic system for energy. Typically there is a brief (5 to 30 seconds) spurt of intense effort in running after and striking the ball followed by a short (10 to 30 seconds) rest while retrieving the ball an awaiting a serve. Then the serve and rally take place and are succeeded by another rest; and so the game goes. The Anaerobic system is under constant demand to provide the necessary ATP for energy. So much for theory.

In part two *Interval Training* lists seventeen major sports and example interval training programs (ITP's) for each. For unknown reasons handball is not included among the seventeen. Under these circumstances the writer has taken the privilege of extrapolating a running program for handball conditioning. This work-out is somewhat analogous to those given for tennis, short distance track events, and lacrosse. The common factor with all these (including handball) is they primarily utilize the Anaerobic energy system.

If the reader is seriously intent upon physical conditioning for handball, say for tournament participation, his running program should include a series of short and middle distance "sprints" with rest between each effort. This is favoured as opposed to a daily five mile run. Long distance running enhances the Aerobic system, which handballers are little concerned with—it is a non-applicable energy system for handball. A satisfactory ITP for handball might be (in ITP lingo):

Set 1 — 4X220 @ :35 (1:45)

2 — 8X110 @ :15 (0:45)

3 — 10X55 @ :10 (0:24)

4 — 6X55 @ :10 (0:24)

In English this translates as four 220 yard runs at 35 seconds with a minute and 45 seconds of rest interval between each run. Now, after set I is completed, eight 110 yard sprints at 15 seconds recovery between each are performed. And so on through four sets. Then collapse. It is important that the rest interval be observed in that it avoids the excessive production of fatigue products. And who wants whatever those are in excess? Generally speaking, the rest interval time should be two to three times the duration of the work time. It should consist of slow jogging or walking.

If the above ITP seems a little too concentrated to the reader, this writer is in concurrence. As an alternative, the use of the interval conditioning can be applied in a more platable manner. For example, if one chooses to run around a track, a suitable work-out might consist of sprinting the straight-aways (work interval) and slow-plodding the curves of the track (relief interval). If running off a track is one's preference, a similar work-out can be attained by travelling the way the Indians used to: run 50 steps and jog or walk 50, run 50, and jog 50...

Part three of *Interval Training* deals with "special consideration", a catch-all title which encompasses an interesting variety of exercise believe-it-or-not type facts, plays a section of self-testing and evaluation. Of special significance to the sweaty court dwellers are the authors' thoughts on salt and water loss: "During strenuous activity, particularly on hot and/or humid days, large amounts of water and some salt are lost by the body. Hear illness can be induced if their replacement does not occur within 24 hours. Water loss is by far the more serious consequence. Unfortunately, the uneducated person concerns himself more with taking salt tables than water. Such is absurd; actually it is a very poor health practice." It is not unusual for a handballer to lose five to ten pounds of water during a blood-and-guts-and-cramps type three game match. A ten pound weight loss is equivalent to 1.25 gallons of water! (One pound equals one pint of water -or perspiration.) The proper way to replace one's water loss is by drinking small amounts of fluid frequently rather than gorging the gut all at once between games. A water or Gatorade jug kept outside the court door is a handy refreshing solution to the problem. This can be referred to during timeouts and floor mopping up episodes.

Gobbling salt tablets without proper water intake is much worse than taking no salt at all. Why is this? Through perspiring we lost more water, comparatively, than salt. Take your average salt pill (7-10 grains). The book recommends that with it you consume a pint (equivalent to two cups-one pound) of water. Note: through testing and evaluation and whatever else the experts do to come up with such figures, it has been found that for the first six pounds of sweat loss, salt tablets are not required; salt obtained previously through the normal diet is sufficient. Gatorade, that lime-coloured sweat (carbonated or non-carbonated), is an entirely acceptable body water replacer. This and other less familiar liquid replacements on the market today allow a person to almost "drink sweat". When consuming these, salt tablets must not be taken.

Keep in mind, Fox and Mathews later point out, that the warmer the day the larger the amount of water loss. A more humid environment (ever play in an enclosed court near an indoor swimming pool on a muggy day?) greatly increases body fluid depletion. Remember, too, that wearing an excess amount of clothing, such as sweatsuits, during play restricts the evaporative cooling are of the skin. The same is true for tight fitting shirts or shorts, tape, etc.

Interval Training: Conditioning for Sports and General Fitness is recommended for handball players as well as participants in any sports requiring moderate to extreme physical exertion. It is also well suited for the "health nut" desiring to condition himself simply for health purposes. Except for the first chapter on the energy systems, which is necessarily technical and detailed, the concept of Interval Training is direct, well presented and easily understood. The book may be obtained by writing the W.B. Saunders Co., W. Washington Square, Philadelphia, PA 19105. The cost is $5.95.

Handball game of action and recovery

Our level of aerobic fitness is measured by our oxygen uptake capacity. Our oxygen uptake capacity determines how soon and how long we must work anaerobically (without sufficient oxygen) in the intermittent action sports such as handball, tennis, soccer, hockey, football, basketball and baseball.

Each liter per minute of oxygen we can take into the muscle cells enables us to do approximately 5 calories of aerobic work. Oxygen uptake is also expressed in militers per kilogram of body weight, per minute. Because it adjusts for variations in body weight, it is a more precise fitness index. For example, a 154 pound (70K.) person who has an oxygen uptake of 3 liters per minute would have an uptake of 42 ml./ K/minute. Whereas a 220 pond (100K.) person with a 3 liter per minute oxygen uptake would have a 30 ml/ K/minute uptake.

Dr. Kenneth Cooper states in *The New Aerobics*. 'That a man less than 29 years of age in good physical condition can process upward of 42.5 ml. of oxygen per kilogram per minute, while a person in very poor condition can process only 25 ml. or less."

Time, distance and weight are the main factors that determine our work load and thus our caloric expenditure. Therefore, in an even match, the 220 pound athlete not only performs more work, but more anaerobic work than his 154 pound opponent.

As both the 154 and 220 pound contestants have a 3 liter oxygen uptake they both can sustain approximately 15 calories of aerobic work per minute. Energy they expend in excess of 15 calories per minute must then be supplemented by one of both of the anaerobic energy systems. Namely, the ATP-PC and/ or Lactic Acid system.

The ATP-PC system is the energy source we use to perform our most intensive work. Energy expended under this system is the energy source we use to perform our most intensive work. Energy expended under this system can go as high as 40 to 50 calories per minute. But the duration of this work is only from a fraction of a second to 10 seconds. The intensive of the work performed under this system is so great that we practically work 100% anaerobically—without oxygen. Consequently, an oxygen debt can build up so quickly that we must stop and make immediate repayment to survive.

In handball, the ATP-PC system would probably energize such actions as the cannon ball serve, kill, and drive shot attempts. Also all animal quick lunges, dashes, stops, and reverse maneuvers. In an hour of singles handball possibly only 20 to 80 seconds will be energized by the ATP-PC system.

As we only have approximately a 10 second store of this animal energy in our muscles at the beginning of the game, it must be continuously replaced during periods of inaction. Fox and Mathews in *Internal Training* (Saunders 1974) state that during a 10 second recovery period practically none of this animal energy substance (phosphocreatine) is re-synthesized in the muscles. But during a 30 second recovery interval 50% of the phosphocreatine is replaced and in 120 seconds approximately 94% is restored. Therefore, during a 30 second time out some of the spring is restored to our muscles which enables us to perform additional high intensity ATP-PC energy work.

The Lactic Acid System takes over to provide energy expended in excess of that which can be provided by our oxygen uptake or aerobic system. An oxygen debt also builds up under the lactic acid energy system. For this reason it also is an anaerobic system of energy production. The duration of work in this system is from 15 seconds to 3 minutes. As this system produces a build up of lactic acid in the blood, it will in a period of two to three minutes practically stop muscle contraction.

Some examples of handball actions that could be energized under the L/A system would be rallies of 15 seconds duration or longer. Also those serves and returns that are more a defensive than an offensive maneuver. A play for position rather than an all out attempt to shoot for the ace, or kill.

Caloric expenditure in the L/A system would probably cover a range of 10 to 30 calories per minute.

Our third energy source is the aerobic or oxygen system. Here the oxygen uptake into the muscle cells is sufficient to furnish the energy needed to perform the level of work without incurring a heavy lactic acid build up in the blood. Unlike the two anaerobic systems mentioned earlier, little to no oxygen debt is incurred when we work aerobically. The caloric expenditure under the aerobic system probably lies in a range of 4 to 17 calories per minute depending upon our oxygen uptake capacity.

Some of the handball actions that are likely to be energized aerobically are: The soft lob serve; front court fly shots dropped into the corner; and balls that can be played long off the back wall. Most of the other times you are playing long off the back wall. Most of the other times you are playing the ball would probably be energized anaerobically. The time your opponent is returning or serving would also be anaerobic for him but it could well be considered aerobic time for you; because you also work while he is playing the ball but not as intense as when you serve or return.

The last energy category in the intermittent action type sports, such as handball, would be the recovery time. Recovery time for handball covers the time from the end of one play until the ball is again served. We also expend calories during the recovery period but probably only in a range of 2 to 4 calories per minute, depending upon the intensity of the previous action. It is during these 10 to 15 seconds of recovery that we try to repay our outstanding oxygen debt.

The opposite to recovery time would be the action time. This is the actual time that the ball is in play. Like recovery time, it can be readily determined with the aid of a stop watch. The number of minutes of action time in an hour of play determines the energy variation from one game to the next.

An hour of competitive single handball that would have 25 minutes of action time could well expend in the neighbourhood of 480 to 500 calories for a 154 pound person. With a drop in the action content of the hour to 20 minutes, his energy expenditure would possibly drop to around 420 to 430 calories for the hour.

Any increase or decrease in the action minutes during the hour of play most likely results in more than a proportionate increase or decrease in anaerobic relative to aerobic expenditure.

Anaerobic energy expenditure produces a high level of work stress. Stress is good or bad depending on how much we must withstand during a given period of time. Stress builds us up or tears us down depending upon our stress resistance level by submitting to gradually increased increments of stress to which we are able to adapt.

Success in the intermittent action sports depends primarily on the factors of skill, experience, physical fitness and motivation. But when opponents are relatively equally matched in skill and experience, fitness and motivation become the deciding factors for success. The will to win weakness with the onset of fatigue because motivation is a physiological as well as a psychological phenomenon.

As mentioned at the beginning and bears repeating: *Our oxygen uptake capacity determines how soon and how long we must work anaerobically in the intermittent action sports such as handball.* The higher our oxygen uptake capacity the longer we are able to work aerobically. Consequently, the lower our oxygen debt and lactic acid accumulation will be. Of equal importance, our oxygen uptake level determines our speed of oxygen debt repayment and recovery during the brief seconds between action.

The intermittent action sports require both strong aerobic and anaerobic energy production systems. Our aerobic capability is best strengthened by performing steady state endurance work of 2 miles or more.

As competitive singles handball is interval training at its best, such participation is probably the best exercise we can do to strengthen our anaerobic capability, developing our skill and experience in the process.

Previously we estimated that a 154-pound athlete, playing an hour of singles handball, having

25 minutes of action time, would expend in the neighbourhoods of 480 to 500 calories.

We will not attempt to roughly estimate the type and amount of fuel he would have consumed to furnish the 480 to 500 calories of energy. To do this requires a breakdown of his total energy expenditure into his three energy production systems. This energy allocation is necessary as the ATP-PC system is fuelled by phosphocreatine; the lactic acid system is fueled solely by carbohydrate; and the aerobic system is fueled by both carbohydrate and serum fats.

To further complicate the task, the lactic acid system only delivers approximately 0.30 calories of energy for each gram of carbohydrate metabolized. Whereas aerobic metabolism uses carbohydrate as energy fuel at 4 calories per gram. Serum fats cannot be metabolized anaerobically as energy fuel. But aerobic metabolism of serum fats provides energy at 9 calories per gram.

During the first hour of aerobic metabolism approximately 50% of the calories expended are fueled by carbohydrate and 50% by serum fats. The fuel contribution of carbohydrate falls off considerably in the second hour of aerobic work and the consumption of serum fats rises to supply the difference.

Assume that in an hour of handball there are 25 minutes of action time at which 1 minute is ATP-PC system work at a rate of 40 cal/min. These 40 calories would be fueled by phosphocreatine. The remaining calories expended during the contest would be fueled by carbohydrate and serum fats.

Of the 24 minutes of action time remaining 1

figure that half, or in this case, 12 minutes would be lactic acid (L/A) expenditure and 12 minutes is aerobic expenditure. Figuring the 12 minutes of L/A expenditure at a rate of 22 cal/min. amounts to 264 calories. But a large portion of this L/A would be aerobic. As our subject athlete has a 3 liter per minute oxygen up-take his aerobic work during these 12 minutes is approximately 180 calories. (3 liters × 5 × 12 min. = 180 calories). Subtracting these 180 calories from the 264 L/A calories leaves a net L/A expenditure of 84 calories.

Finally, the aerobic system expenditure was figured in as follows: The remaining 12 minutes of action time @10 cal/min. for 120 calories; plus the 180 aerobic calories expended in the L/A system; and the 35 minutes of recovery time at 2 cal/min. for 70 calories. This makes the total aerobic expenditure 370 calories.

This breakdown now enables us to chart the approximate energy and fuel expenditure for:

One hour of singles Handball having 25 minutes of action time

By a 154 pound athlete with a 3 liter per/min. oxygen up-take

Approximate Energy Expended in Calories By Energy Systems Approximate Energy Expended in Calories By Energy Systems		Approximate Fuel Consumed in Grams Carbohydrates— Serum Fats Approximate Fuel Consumed in Grams	
		Carbohydrates —	Serum Fats
ATP-PC System			
1 min. @40 cal/min..............	40	0	0
LA System			
12 min. @22 cal/min. =	264		
Minus aerobic portion			
3 liters x 5 x 12 min.—	180		

Net L/A..............................	84	84 ÷ 0.3 = 280		
Aerobic System				
12 min. @10 cal/min. =	120			
Aerobic portion of L/A =	180			
35 min. of recovery time				
2/cal/min. =	70			
Total aerobic.....................	370	÷ 2 = 185	46	÷ 185 9 = 20
		÷ 4.0 = 46		20
Total expenditure..............	494	(calories)	326 (grams)	20 (grams)

According to the American Association for Health, Physical Education and Recreation a 154 pound person, in good physical condition, has the following normal carbohydrate storage:

250 grams of muscle glycogen
15 grams of blood sugar
110 grams of liver glycogen

This is a total reserve of 375 grams of carbohydrate (glycogen and blood sugar). But fatigue will undoubtedly set in before we ever completely expend this reserve. Figuring a 95% rate of depletion, our athlete would have 356 grams available by 5.4 we could place his estimated onset of fatigue at approximately 66 minutes of playing time.

However, if our subject athlete had only a 2½ rather than a 3 liter per minute oxygen up-take, his net lactic acid system expenditure would have been 114 rather than 84 calories; and his total aerobic expenditure would have been 340 rather than 370 calories. Consequently, his hourly carbohydrate consumption would have been 422 grams, or 7 grams per minute. This rate of carbohydrate expenditure would place his estimated time of fatigue at approximately 76 minutes of playing time.

Comparing handball with distance running

emphasizes the fuel inefficiency of intermittent action, relative to steady state work. For example, our 154-pound athlete in running 7½ miles per hour (8 min/ mile would use approximately 750 calories in an hour. But as he would be working close to 100% aerobically he would only consume 93 grams of carbohydrate. This is 3½ times less carbohydrate than he expends in one hour of handball.

Furthermore, the hour of distance running would use 41.33 grams of serum fats, which is twice as much as the hour of handball. Possibly this is one reason why handball players generally weigh more than distance runners.

Some people may question the expenditure of 280 grams of carbohydrates to fuel only 84 calories of lactic acid system energy work. Therefore going into some detail on the anaerobic metabolic process may help one better understand this comparatively excessive fuel expenditure.

When we work aerobically a unit of carbohydrate is fully oxidized through a number of chemical steps on a long ladder that ultimately ends up as carbon and water molecules. In aerobic metabolism one unit of carbohydrate produces 38 ATP energy units.

However, when we work anaerobically a unit of carbohydrate is only partially oxidized. It is converted to lactic acid which is only the next chemical step in the energy ladder. Lactic acid production releases only 2 ATP energy units per unit of carbohydrate.

During a few hours of recovery approximately 85% of this lactic acid buildup is converted by the liver, back into glucose or glycogen. This reconverted liver glycogen will then be available to energize tomorrow's game. But regardless of this future conversation, anaerobic metabolism in today's game continues to excessively draw down our limited store of carbohydrate.

Our muscles can use either serum fats or carbohydrate for energy fuel. But the brain and the rest of our central nervous system depends solely on carbohydrate for energy fuel. One type of molecule, called GABA (which is necessary for the regulation of the brain) can only be synthesized from carbohydrate.

When we either run low of liver glycogen, or cannot convert it into glucose fast enough to meet our rate of expenditure, our blood sugar level quickly becomes exhausted. Sustaining a high level of mental and nervous system is all but impossible. Result is hypoglycemic stress or low blood sugar.

The normal carbohydrate level of the blood is approximately 1 gram per liter of blood or 100 mg/100 ml. A drop to ½ grap per liter of blood or 50 mg/100 ml. brings on server hypoglycemia.

The symptoms of low blood sugar are: muscle coordination deteriorates, concentration becomes increasingly difficult, mental reactions are slowed, emotional control is lessened, motivation is weakened and confidence gives way to doubt. This condition describes and is referred to as depression or fatigue.

Fatigue, ultimately, is to the brain and the central nervous system. For athletes with a hypoglycemic tendency, fatigue can set in even when there is sufficient muscle glycogen remaining to energize their physical action. But normal exercise fatigue results when the demand from depleted muscle glycogen is competing with the demand of the central nervous system and brain for blood sugar.

In either case the rate of release of liver glycogen (glucose) into the blood is not adequate to meet the total energy expenditure and hypoglycemic stress results. Hypoglycemic stress is then interpreted by the brain as fatigue.

Weight training for Handball

Handball is an enjoyable, fast-moving game which requires a high degree of motor skills, mental concentration, and physical ability. While there are several factors which affect the amount of improvement which can be attained in either motor skills or mental concentration, the literature is replete with conditioning programs purporting to improve personal physical fitness. One of the more common techniques included in such self-improvement programs is the use of progressive resistance training—weight training.

Unfortunately, despite its wide acceptance as a potentially valuable conditioning tool, weight lifting (as an activity) is frequently plagued by misconceptions, misapplications, and ill-founded habits. If your goal is to improve your handball ability by means of a weight training program, your initial task is to organize a program which is sound, functional, and efficient. It is sound if it is based on scientific principles. It is functional if the strength developed is specific to the objectives of the program. It is efficient if it produces the desired results in the shortest period of time possible.

For the layman, he can develop a weight training program which is reasonably scientifically sound if attention is given to the seven basic strength training variables:

(1) *Reps*—Maximum gains in strength can be obtained by performing 8-12 repetitions of each exercise. If you can perform less than eight reps, the weight is too heavy, more than 12, the weight is too light. Add more weight when you can perform 12 repetitions of any exercise.

(2) *Sets*—There is no need to perform more than two sets of any exercise. Two sets of a properly performed exercise will produce maximum efficiency. The key to any exercise program is the quality of the exercise and not the quantity. Strive to exert a maximum effort on each set of each exercise. Try to reach the point where you can no longer perform a properly executed repetition (for maximum efficiency this should take place between the 8th and the 12th repetition).

(3) *Workload*—Emphasize the overload principle. Strive to make your muscles work harder each time by using more weight or performing more repetitions. For maximum efficiency, use as much weight as you can handle to properly perform 8-12 repetitions.

(4) *Time Interval*—The time interval between the first and second set of the same exercise should be somewhere between 30 seconds and 1½ minutes. The time interval between different exercises should be as much as you need to recover adequately from the previous exercise so that you will be capable of exerting a maximum effort.

(5) *Frequency of Workouts*—For maximum efficiency, the frequency of workout should be three times per week while alternating days. Emphasize the law of use and disuse. When a muscle is used (overload principle) it will hypertrophy (grow bigger and stronger). When it is not used, it will atrophy (grow smaller and weaker). For a muscle to continue to hypertrophy, it must be exercised every 48-72 hours or it will gradually begin to workout. Inversely, a muscle needs 48-72 hours to completely recover from exercise. To exercise any sooner would not allow adequate recovery or maximum increases in strength. Irregular workouts will not produce significant gains in strength. The best organized program will not significantly increase your strength if it is not performed regularly (3x/week). It should be emphasized that the first few months of any exercise program are probably the most important. To skip a workout during this period could set the individual back two to three workouts.

(6) *Order of Exercise*—The order of exercise for maximum efficiency should be as follows:

a. Legs

b. Torso

c. Arms

d. Abdominals

The legs are exercised first because they possess the greatest potential for gaining strength. They are also the largest muscle groups in the body. When exercising the muscles of the torso, you should alternate pressing and pulling movements. When performing any pressing movement you are utilizing the pectorals, deltoids, and triceps. When performing any pulling movement, the last and biceps are employed. Therefore, by alternating a pressing and pulling movement, it will allow the opposing muscle groups adequate time to recover.

The muscles of the arms should be exercised after, not before, the muscles of the torso. The muscles of the arms (biceps-triceps) are much smaller and weaker than the larger and stronger muscles of the torso. The muscles of the arms assist when performing all of the exercises for the torso. To fatigue the smaller and weaker muscles of the arms first would result in a non-productive workout for the larger and stronger muscles of the torso.

For example, the primary muscles used to perform a pullup are the lats and the biceps. If you were to fatigue the biceps and then attempt to perform pullups or chinups, you would be unable to perform anywhere near the number of reps needed to strengthen the larger and potentially stronger lats. However, by reversing the order, you can obtain maximum efficiency for both exercises.

(7) *Exercises to be performed*—There are a variety of exercises from which to choose from. For a general strength development program you should select multi-joint or compound exercises. That is to select an exercise that will facilitate an increase in strength of the major muscle groups of the body. For specific strength development, select exercises which will develop the musculature involved in the skills you wish to improve. Although handball is a game requiring a total body effort, the arms, legs,

and shoulder-girdle area play a particularly important role.

When organizing a weight training program to improve the musculature involved in performing a specific handball skill (e.g., ceiling shot), use the following procedures:

(1) Observe and analyse the movement. (e.g., ceiling shot).

(2) Determine what the major muscles or the prime movers are involved in executing that particular event. (e.g., latissimus dorsi, deltoids, triceps, forearm flexors).

(3) Prescribe specific exercises to strengthen the muscles used to perform that activity. (e.g., lat pulldown, seated press, triceps extension, wrist curls).

If maximum results are to be attained, it is essential that proper lifting techniques be emphasized:

(1) Raise the weight without using moment (no bouncing or jerking movements).

(2) Emphasize the lowering of the weight (take longer to lower the weight than you did to raise it).

(3) Do not sacrifice form to increase the weight or repetitions. One final consideration involves periodic evaluation. You should continually monitor your progress so that appropriate adjustments can be made (whenever necessary) to insure that your program is successful. Given all of the aforementioned, add a touch of personal dedication, and watch your game improve.

5

HOW TO HIT A HANDBALL

Just as the universe is made up of atoms, your handball game is made up of strokes, hundreds of individual swings of the arm. The quality of those individual swings determines the overall quality of your game, just as the nature of individual atoms determines whether a substance is gold or feathers. Therefore it is all important that you learn a sound fundamental handball swing before you start to compete in matches.

One is reminded of Ted Williams when an adoring fan asked him what made him such a great hitter: "Two things," he said, "a willingness to work and attention to detail.

Jim Jacobs, perhaps the greatest four waller of them all, recounts how he used to spend hours in front of a length mirror examining his stroke, trying to detect flaws that robbed him of power and accuracy.

Good handball players all have good handball swings. But if you go to a tournament players all have good players, the first thing you will notice is they all have unique swings; they all seem to do it little differently. You'll find yourself wondering how you can even learn the right way to hit the ball.

Don't despair. The fundamental handball stroke has certain features common to all the good players. Body types styles, and extraneous idiosyncrasies all serve to make handball swings look different. But at several crucial points sound strokes all adhere to the same basic principles.

Body position

The stroke starts with body position. Your swing's effectiveness depends on how well you station yourself to allow a free swinging movement with the arm. Step number one for the sidearm stroke: face the side wall when hitting to the front wall. During a rally, the ferocity of the action tempts a player to flail way at the ball without taking the extra hop step necessary to face the side wall for the stroke.

The reason this step is crucial will become clear when we talk about stepping into the ball and transferring the weight; you can't do these two things when your body faces the front wall; therefore you lose control and power in your shots. Facing the side wall, on the other hand makes stepping into the ball the natural thing to do and as a bonus it makes it much easier to watch the ball rather than the front wall, another important element of a good swing.

So you prepare for the upcoming shot by facing the side wall. Next you must align the body so that when it comes time to actually strike the ball, the and your hand meet at the center line of your body (the center line is where your nose, in chin, and belly button are in case you were wondering). This means you must judge where the center line will be after you take your step into the ball; generally one foot behind the ball is a good place to start your forward movement. Okay, now imagine yourself facing the side wall, a foot behind the ball as it drops into your striking zone (any height that is comfortable between the waist and the knees), and you're ready to swing. As you take your arm back, turn your shoulders back also, then open up your hips and rotate into the ball. Don't worry too much about this shoulder and hip action; it should come naturally. Hitting a handball should feel just like throwing a ball; the body movements the same. Handball players almost always warm-up by taking a few throws against the front wall, because the similar movements prepare their bodies for the more difficult task of hitting the ball. In fact, a good way to practice your swing is to throw an imaginary ball into a full length mirror. Imitate that same throwing motion when you hit the ball.

Leg position

Handball players start to slip when their legs old. This fact alone reliably indicates the importance footwork plays in the handball stroke. You must use your legs to get yourself in position for the shot.

First, the legs get you to the ball so you set up behind it preparatory to stepping into it. Secondly, the legs are the means by which you take that all important single step into the ball as you're hitting it. Through this step comes a very large share of whatever power you generate in the shot.

Proper footwork in hitting a handball is as beautiful as one of Bach's Brandenburg Concertos. The move is trumpeted with several short staccato steps to get in position, and then the smooth, violin-like step into the ball. Legwork makes all the elements of the shot blend together and the picture is one of effortlessness and grace.

Make sure your legs keep you can arm's length away from the ball so the swing remains free and uncramped.

In a sense, legwork initiates the handball stroke by getting your body to the right place on the court. Then comes the cocking of the arm, the backward rotation of the shoulders and hips; then the forward step that opens the hips and commences the forward position of the handball swing.

Many players find a little shuffle step helpful in relaxing and loosening the body for the shot. It serves the same purpose as the forward press in golf or the little hip wiggle some golf teaches suggest to initiate the golf swing. OR you might compare it to the shuffle a short-stop gives his feet after picking up a ground ball before throwing to first; he does it for balance and positioning.

In handball this movement usually consists of a little three-step hop into the ball. The extra steps get the legs moving and make the final step into the ball that much easier and much more fluid. It is a movement that helps especially on fly shots where getting set up properly needs to be done very quickly and so is partially difficult. If you practice this little three-step movement you'll find it feels very natural and helpful.

The final step into the ball transfers the weight from your back foot to your front foot at the same time the wrist snaps through the ball. If done properly, it all comes together for a firm, solid shot. This perfect feel when everything comes through at the same time is called good timing.

Head position

During the entire stroke the head points directly towards the handball. Don't neglect this point. If one element of the swing can be called crucial or ultra-essential, watching the ball is it. No swing succeeds without watching the ball.

Solid head position helps the swing for two reasons. The first is obvious: if you don't see the ball, you can't hit it. The golfing advice that you should see the clubface strike the back of the ball holds true for handball as well: you should see your glove cone into the back of the handball.

Secondly, a solid steady head provides a fulcrum around which the rest of the body turns. Simple physics tells us that speed increases momentum. In order to generate the most power in your swing it is necessary to get your arm and hand moving as fast as possible. Swinging the arm and trunk around a fixed axis increases the speed of the swing which leads directly to greater power.

Think of the body as a spinning top. The center of the top barely moves; the outside of the top must move very fast to keep up. OR think of your hand as the end of a golf club; it must swing very fast to keep up with the slower moving parts of the body nearer to the center axis such as the shoulder.

What happens if the head moves forwards? The speed of the arm is decreased because it doesn't have to move quite so fast to whip around the head. Thus, if you lunge at the ball in an attempt to hit it harder, you're actually defeating your purpose; the arm will travel slower, and as a result the ball travel slower.

A problem beginning ball players often have is trying to watch both the ball and the front wall, the place where they are aiming. You can't do both. The experienced ballplayer rarely looks at the front wall. He is either watching the ball for his own shot or watching his opponent hit the ball. One thing he does, however, is to imagine the front wall. In his mind he "sees" the area of the front wall he wants to hit and his this visualization helps guide the shot to that area. This kind of mental practice has good documentation by psychologists who have performed numerous experiments showing that mental imaging of a desired result acts positively towards achieving that result. So keep the head still on the outside but active on the inside.

Hand position

It all comes down to the hands; it should in a game called handball. Actually, it all comes down to a specific of the hands the hitting area. The ideal hitting area is surprisingly small-an area roughly the size of the handball on the top part of the palm at the base of the two middle fingers. Good players hit the ball there almost all the time and have the callouses to prove it.

Five-time national champion Paul Haber has a callous on his right hand that has become legendary. Paul's big trick in bars, where he spends an inordinate amount of his time, was to extinguish his cigarettes on the palm of his hand, protected of course by his callous. This trick won Paul many drinks, another advertisement for the virtues of handball.

Hitting the ball in the sweet spot takes practice. It's difficult task and will only come after long, hard practice. But it really pays off in terms of control. The actual contact of hand and ball is not so much a collision as a caress. It is accomplished with a cupped hand, a position that lessens the impact of the ball and softens what can otherwise be a jarring joining. After the ball strikes the sweet spot it usually rolls up off the end of the fingers or off the side of the hand. Which way it rolls determines the kind of spin the ball will have.

During the stroke the hands and wrists should be loose and relaxed. This makes the snap of the wrist impact much more pronounced. As the arm swings the hand down into the ball, the elbow leads the way; it reaches the centerline of the body before the hand. When the elbow reaches the plane of the ball, then the wrist and forearm snap the hand forward at tremendous speed. Remember speed equals power. The rest of the swing is a natural follow through.

Another very popular method of hitting the ball is with the fist. The hand is fisted and the ball is struck on the cuticles of the two middle fingers. The first stroke is accomplished with a stiff wrist, and the power in the shot comes from the shoulder and the relatively hard surface off which the ball rebounds, the clenched hand.

Because the mechanics of the fist are much simpler a than the free swinging open-handed shot, it is very popular for use with the off-hand. Its major drawback is a marked loss of control.

6

OFFENSIVE STRATEGIES

One of the most important decisions to be made by a top ball players as he moves into position to attempt a shot is whether to go on the "offense" or "defense". By making the correct decision these articles—*Playing the percentages!* Offense is that time when you have the opportunity to hit a rally ending kill or pass shot. So, when is that time? As a rule, you should consider yourself to be "on the offense" whenever you have time to come to a complete stop before attempting your shot, you can stroke the ball from a comfortable position below your waist and especially when you can do so with your strong hand. The last part of the preceding statement brings up a much debated topic.

Offensive off-hand?

The question in the debate is, "Do you have to be hit kill shots with your off-hand?" we don't think so. We believe you must be able "to defense" with you off-hand. By that we mean you must hit the ball in such a manner that it will drive your opponent to a point very close to the back wall. From this court position. It will be very difficult for him to hit an offensive kill or pass.

Three of our greatest National Champions, Jim Jacobs, Paul Haber and Fred Lewis played mostly "defense" with their off-hands. We recently re-read a letter Jim Jacobs wrote to me over 15 years ago. In it he said that prior to 1955 he was "left hand crazy"—that he attempted all kinds of spectacular kills with his off-hand; although he succeeded quite often, he lost the big important matches. He then decided to change his thinking and developed his "Sword and Shield Theory" in which he considered his off-hand to be his "shield," mainly defensive with no mistakes. His right hand became his "sword". When he decided to go on the offensive, it would be with his strong hand. Jimmy went on to say that when the defeated the great Vic Hershkowitz in the National Finals in 1955, he scored *Not one point* with his left hand, but he *only missed 4 shots the entire match!* In changing his game, Jacobs became a less spectacular player but he also became the Number One player in the game for ten years.

Now we know you can counter this argument by asking "What about Dennis Hofflander? Are you trying to tell us that Dennis should not be attempting kill shots with his left hand? Our answer is "if you can hit kill shots kill Dennis can as often as he can then do it!" The great majority of us will never be able to hit the great offensive shots with our off-hands as often as Dennis can, but all of us can learn to "defense" with our off-hands and do it very well.

When you start discussing the great offensive off-hands of players like Hofflander, Buzz Shumate etc. You need to define what is meant by percentages in "offensive" handball. What these articles are attempting to relate is how to play the best percentage game according to your position on the court and the position of the ball in relation of the body (height Closeness to the body, strong or weak hand, etc.) For example, skill shot attempt with your strong and 20 feet away from the front wall should be a higher percentage shot than one hit with your off-hand from 30 feet away. The further you are from the front wall, the less your chances of hitting an accurate offensive shot; and keep in mind that offensive shots do require great accuracy. Also if you must hit a ball from above the waist you have less of a chance to make a good kill shot than if you had attempted your shot from around knee height.

When Paul Haber hits his favourite right corner kill from deep court with his off-hand, he is going against the "court percentages," but because he is so fantastically accurate with that particular shot, it is a percentage shot for him. This we refer to as *personal percentage.* Many players have a shot or two that fits this "personal percentage" category. So if you can hit a kill shot with your off-hand from 35 feet away, and if you can make this shot 7 or 8 times out of 10 attempts go ahead and use it. It is one of the your personal percentage shots. You should recognize, however, that you will have days when you don't your shots as accurately as you would like and no those days you should eliminate these higher risk "personal percentage" shots and start attempting the best percentage shot based on your court position—*court percentages.*

You should also know that your percentages may change during a game. Spectacular shots that you can make a high percentage of the time when you are fresh can easily become low percentage shots when you are tired. Stuffy Singer, who is a fine teacher as well as great ballplayer says the will often play games after working out so he is tired when he starts playing. By doing this he can analyse his game and discover which of his many great shots are still high percentage shots when he becomes tired and which are not. He then decides to eliminate the low percentage shots whenever he gets to a point in a match when he becomes tried. If you try this it could mean you should eliminate over half of your shots when you are tired especially if those shots begin finding the floor first instead of the bottom board. Remember, most of your really important matches will be won or lost when you are tried! It is no wonder the players who have really dominated this game were those with the great defensive shots they never missed. It is not easy to hit kill shots from 38 feet away when you are fresh much less when you are tired at the end of a long tough match.

At the beginning of this chapter we said that the most important decision you must make when attempting your shot is whether or not to go on offense. All right, let's say you are set and you can hit the ball from below the waist with your strong hand; now you make the correct decision to go on offense. What do you do? Should you attempt a kill" Straight or corner? May be a pass? Which kind of pass? A corner kill shot is a fine shot. Let's say you attempt it and hit a beautiful shot is a inches high, but your opponent digs it up and passes you. Now what are your thoughts? Perhaps "if hit it lower he won't get in next time!? " *Wrong!!* If you can hit that kill shot four inches high you have doe all that is necessary for success—*physically*. But to do what is necessary for success *Mentally*, you must understand percentages as they relate to offensive shot selections. Then you will understand why a "good" shot is not necessarily an "effective" shot.

In order for your offensive shot to be effective the ball must hit the floor twice before your opponent can reach it. So the first question you need to ask yourself as you are about to attempt your shot is "where is my opponent?" How would you know where to angle your shot it don't know where he is ? Is he in front court deep court left court, left, right or center? You can't pass your opponent if he is in deep court, and it's very difficult to kill the ball into the corner if he is standing up close to the front wall. What happens if you don't execute perfectly? Jim Jacobs who always had a unique way of getting your attention said that....."Whenever you attempt a kill shot assume you are going to miss it! By this he meant you should assume your kill shot attempt will hit the front wall 12 inches high instead of 3 inches high. If this happens will your shot still be a difficult one for your opponent to retrieve? If the answer is yes then you are playing with your head as well as with your hands. This is percentage handball!

Another question you need to answer is where are you when you attempt your shot? Are you in center or close to a side wall? Are you close to the front wall or close to the shot you choose because certain shots are just too difficult to make when the ball is in deep court, especially when the ball is very close to a side wall. The closer you are to the front wall and center of the court the better your chances of greater accuracy with a wider selection of good shot according to your opponent's position, but from your position it may be too difficult to hit a high percentage of the time; so you should select another good shot you have a better chance of making.

Another important question that must be answered is what shot did you attempt last time when you and your opponent's court positions were similar? Don't attempt the same offensive shot every time from the same place. Give your opponent credit for a memory. He will start "over-playing" your shot which will allow him to retrieve a well hit ball. You should as you have no doubt heard someone say, Mix 'Em Up! For every possible positioning of the players there are two three and sometimes four good, high percentage shot selections.

This "mixing 'em up" was one of the things that made players like Singer, Jacobs Lewis Johnny Sloan and Ken Schneider so very effective. Once you gave the offensive opportunity, you did not know where they are going to hit it which made their opponents hesitate. This hesitation allowed these great players to score with shots that weren't perfectly hit. This is also playing the percentages. It allows you to hit winners even when you are not executing your best. If you have to hit a perfect shot to score, you are making the wrong shot selection.

Still another very important question to be answered is who are you playing? What are the strengths and weaknesses of that particular opponents? If possible this should be answered before you begin the game. Sometimes watch your opponents play and attempt to discover their "favourite" shot while picking out weaknesses. Have a game plan before you start the game. Would you try to out-kill a Hofflander or out-volley a Lewis or Haber? You might try but don't expect to get many points! Attempt to play with your "strengths" and force your opponent to play with his particular "weaknesses."

Kill shot strategy

As a general rule, when attempting kill shots try to hit the front corners when your opponent is in rear court. You should usually attempt to hit the side wall first so if the shot is hit a little high it will rebound to the opposite side wall, and may still be difficult shot to retrieve. Corner kill shot attempts that hit the front wall first will rebound to center court if hit too high, and this is what you want to avoid. Keep your shots from rebounding down the middle.

When your opponent is in front court try to hit straight front wall kill shots angled so they will rebound close to a side wall. Hit these shots very hard and even if you hit these shots a little high they may still be effective. Of course there will always be exceptions to these general rules Fred-Lewis often attempts corner kills that contact the front wall first and he is successful a high percentage of the time because that particular shot happens to be of his high "personal percentage" shots.

Pass shot strategy

Sometimes when watching good young players it seems all they ever do is attempt kill shots on the offense. Passing shots are accidental or only used occasionally in very obvious situations. Don't be misled by the "Box score" of the top pro matches. For example the box score of a typical game played by Fred Lewis might read: Kill shots-15 and pass shots-4

By looking at this you might believe the pass shot

is not as important as the kill; but what this box score shows is how the relies were won, not how many kills and passes were attempted. If it showed attempts, it might read: *kill shots*-20 and *pass shots* -50 !!A!

You will not score as often with the pass shot-directly; but indirectly, they wear your opponent down force him into giving you setups, and keep him off-balance which allows you to score easier with your kill shot attempts.

There are three types of pass shots. This is a rather obvious shot that can be attempted whenever your opponent gives you a set-up in center court. It should (As well pass shots should) be hit very hard and low enough so it will not be playable off the back wall. Of course just how high will depend on your own particular power.

The two-wall or "V" pass is an excellent shot because it is more deceptive. The ball should rebound from the front wall and contact the side wall slightly behind your opponent before hitting the floor. This shot is usually hit higher than the one-wall pass, because it will lose speed after hitting the side wall. Again just how high you hit these shots will depend on the height you contact the ball and your power. If Steve August were to hit a one-wall pass that contacted the front wall two feet high, it would probably come off the back wall for a setup!

The third type of pass is the "Slider". This is a one-wall pass that rebounds from the front wall and strikes the floor very close to a side wall; because of the "English" imparted to the ball when you hit the shot "straightens out" and runs down the side wall.

This shot can be hit down the same side wall as the hand with which you contact the ball if you put "natural English" on the ball-right hand down the right side wall and left hand down the left side wall. You can also hit these "sliders" down the opposite side wall if you are able to put "reverse English" on the ball.

Its very important to be able to execute offensive shots; anyone can learn them with enough concentrated practice. And it is just as important to make the correct shot selection—*play the percentages!*

7

FOOTWORK

Footwork is the most important in almost any sport you can name. Because handball is mainly a running game, the importance of good footwork proper conditions of the and legs and of getting into the right court position are of evident importance and all are intertwined.

Face the ball when you hit it..... If the ball is coming down the right wall, face the right wall. If it's is coming down the left side, face left. If you re taking it off the back wall, face the back wall, pivoting as you swing.

Now if its coming straight at you from the wall shift your feet as you'll be facing right or left as you start your swing.

Keep moving....Don't ever stop. In other words don't ever come to a dead stop and plant yourself. And particularly don't ever let your weight get on your heels-keep it on the balls of your feet. By this I do not mean on your toes, or you'll over-balance.

Special exercise

Try this exercise...with your weight on the balls of your feet, move to your left with short steps moving slowly. Then make a sudden take off to your right. You will plant your left foot hard and drive off it to change direction. But because you had some motion the change of direction is easier.

You can change direction faster you can start from a dead stop. By getting into position you can stroke the ball rather than bat at it stab at it.

If you hit a ceiling shot deep in the back court, you can be reasonably certain that your opponent (If he hasn't moved up to take it on the fly) will hit a high return. But you don't know for sure. And you don't know whether he'll hit it down the left or right or whether he'll give you a twist shot out of the corner. He might even drive it low along either wall.

There's only one way you can anticipate where you should be for his return and that is to watch the ball until he has hit it. Then you may have to turn your back on the ball to into position-but never take your eyes off the ball or your opponent until he has swung.

Too many players make their break before the other player has hit, which brings me to another point. Never commit yourself in any direction at full speed.

If you had to move close to the back wall for a shot for example you naturally want to get back to center, front court to be ready for anything. But drift back, for as soon as you break fast, your opponent will cross you up catch you "on the wrong foot" as they say in tennis, and drive the ball behind you.

In this connection here's tip that may be of value. If you have to go to any wall at full-speed for a get, sometimes you save time by taking an extra step or two and then pushing yourself off the wall. It is frequently faster than trying to brake yourself stop, and start back. This may come under the heading of court strategy rather than footwork but I'd like to point out that as the national championship matches near the final rounds, you see fewer and fewer players on the floor.

Dive is wasted

The best players have figured out that you can run to the ball faster than you can dive for it—if keep your feet moving and keep your balance properly distributed. I can honestly say I've never fallen down in the court unless my foot slipped on some perspiration and I've never dived for a ball. You can get there faster with your feet than with you body.

In this connection you will find—if you will believe it-that there's hardly a ball hit that can't be retrieved. You be played some baseball no doubt and you must have amazed yourself at least once by catching a fly on the dead run that you thought you couldn't reach. The same thing happens in handball. The ball "hung" for that split possible returns if you persevere.

Proper foot action

The object of footwork is to get into position to stroke your shot. Now then, what should your foot action be when actually hitting the ball? It's about the same action you use playing catch with a baseball. Your whole back foot is on the floor as you begin to swing, with your right hand, with the forward toe just touching the floor. As you swing the weight is transferred naturally and smoothly from the back foot to the forward one, with the forward foot coming into full contact with the floor as power is applied you hit "against" the leading foot just as you do with a baseball or golf swing. On almost every shot the knees should be flexed slightly-more for low shots of course.

Keep weight forward

The most important thing is that your weight on the balls of your feet, even though the entire foot is in contact with the floor. This does not means it should be on your toes, for it your weight is too far forward you will be off-balance and will have a tendency to fall or lunge forward after the shot. You will also lose power. Most handball shots whether overhand sidearm or underhand are more than an action of the hand and wrist. The whole arm, the shoulders the back the hips the legs-and the feet-come into play.

No matter how much you love the game you can't spend all your time in a handball court-and very few want to. But there are a lot of things you can do outside the court that will prove rewarding and beneficial to your game.

Not many take up acrobatic tap dancing but we still do exercises we learned in those days, and we pass them along here as probably the most beneficial of all for both strengthening and limbering your legs for handball:

- Shallow knee bend of half squat.
- Rise up on the toes.
- Deep knee bends (full squat).

Repeat each exercise in various positions several times. This will develop all the leg muscles in a uniform way, making them strong enough to stand the stresses of handball supple enough to respond to the many positions the game demands.

- For further muscle development coordination and looseness we list here a number of practice suggestions.
- Practising alone with emphasis on facing the ball on very shot.
- Practising along with emphasis on moving at all times with short steps, the weight on the balls of the feet.
- Practising alone to retrieve "hangers". Stand near the left rear corner. Throw the ball into the right front corner six inches to a foot off the floor, then run for it-and don't give up .Vary this with shots from various points-but persevere on every shot.
- To build endurance and to strengthen your legs, running is good. But run a quarter mile or less at a time, *On your toes.* Heel and toe running at long distances will not bring a tenth the benefit of sprints on the toes.
- Ballroom dancing on the balls of your feet, will help you achieve a high standard of footwork. Imagine what handball players Fred Astaire and Gene Kelly would have made if they'd tried.
- Swimming is excellent since it keeps your legs strong and supple, relaxes your muscles and builds endurance. An older player who's relaxed will outlast a stronger, younger opponent who is tense. And remember, one tournament game takes as much out of you as half a dozen practice games because of the tension involved. Practice relaxing and pacing yourself, so you'll do it naturally in competition.

- Other sports. Basketball and soccer are both excellent because of the footwork and strategy involved. Soccer is especially beneficial in Ireland where you are allowed to kick the ball in handball. *Alex Boisseree,* one of the best players in the Los Angeles area, was named soccer player of the year in China before the war (and was interned there thought the war, incidentally).
- During calisthenics in the morning or evening, practice deep knee bends on your toes.
- Finally take care of your feet. Wear one two pairs of heavy wool sweat box. Wear sneakers that have not worn smooth (Some types actually serve as a squeegee if you hit a wet spot on the floor and prevent spills).

8

THE PASS SHOT

An old adage on the professional handball tour maintains that you "kill for show and pass for dough" (golfers recently borrowed this concept, as in "drive for show and putt for dough"). Question the pro handballers further and they'll tell you flat out the majority of the points scored in a game of handball come from pass shots.

This answer flies in the face of what most people would expect. Most players would anticipate the kill shot or the ace serve as the single largest point-getting maneuver. But it's that little ol' down-home-folks pass shot that gives you the consistent winners.

A pass shot is just what the name implies; a ball that travels past your opponent (instead of right at him or in front of him) as it rebounds off the front wall. Players use many different methods to hit the ball past opponents; different strokes, different angles, different speeds, different spins. All aim at one purpose-forcing an opponent who is entrenched in front or middle court to the back court.

Good players simply adore the pass shot, and for good reason. The pass shot holds none of the dangers of the high-risk kill shot. The pass has a much wider margin of error; even if you don't' hit it in precisely the spot you want, the shot sill demands a well-executed return by your opponent.

Furthermore, you can execute the pass shot easily. You don't have to hit it hard, you don't have to bend low or reach high, and you don't have to worry about hitting it into the floor. Players use several different varieties of pass shots: the straight pass, the two wall pass, and the volley pass.

Several verities or principles of use, if followed, make the pass shot the heart and soul of every handball rally. The value of the pass shot becomes clear when you look at all the good things that happen through its use. Once you become convinced of its value, you'll want to practice the pass shot constantly. It will make you a winner.

Varieties

Even beginning players, probably without realizing it, constantly hit the straight pass shot. They usually mis-hit it, mis-direct it, or club it, but they attempt it all the same. Just hitting the ball back to the front wall is a variety of the straight pass, because most players don't try and hit it back at their opponent; they try to hit to one side of him. However, systematic, conscious use of the straight pass is another story. The one thing that marks the passage of a player from the beginning stage of handball to the intermediate stage is the conscious placement of shots. The intermediate player tries to do something with the ball, and when he reaches this stage, the straight pass shot becomes his bread and butter.

Successful straight pass shots travel right down one of two side walls, as close as possible without touching one of them, or as one wag put it "as close as a skinflint sticks to his money." Placement of the ball that close to a side wall forces the opponent to move out of the center court to retrieve the ball, and, it is hoped, all the way to one of the back corners

The straight pass can be hit from any place on the court with either hand, as well as down either side wall. Advanced players put "English" on the ball to make it hug the wall, or as handball author Dick Robertson put it, "fade away along the side wall."

A straight pass hits the front wall and then hits the floor before touching any side wall. It then bounces into one of the rear corners. Only then, on the downward trajectory of the first bounce, might it strike one of the side walls.

In contrast to the straight pass, the two-wall pass hits the front wall and then the side wall on the fly (two walls) before striking the floor, ideally in middle court somewhere behind the short line. Because the angle at which the two-wall pass strikes the front wall resembles the letter V, it is often called a V-pass.

Many players call the two-wall pass the most devastating shot in handball. Whether we would go so far as to call it more devastating than the flat kill or the ace serve is questionable, but the two-wall pass certainly ranks as the most insidious shot in handball because of the cumulative damage it does to your opponent. It literally wears him down.

Thinking ballplayers use the V-pass to score points occasionally when they catch their opponent overplaying the front court, but more often to set up a winning shot two or three exchanges down the line.

Constant use of the two-wall pass can be very damaging to a less disciplined player's psyche.

A third type of pass shot, the volley pass, can be either the straight or the two-wall variety. Volley, of course, means the ball is hit out of the air. Usually the volley in handball surprises the opponent; it startles him when the ball comes back so quickly. In addition, the player who uses the volley shot usually attempts a kill shot off it; a pass attempt of the volley has tremendous effect. Frequently a player, seeing his opponent take the ball out of the air, starts an uncontrolled rush to the front court anticipating a kill attempt. A drive pass shot will catch such a player totally out of position.

Because of the increased tempo of the volley pass shot, the margin of error is even greater than that of the regular pass shot. Sometimes you catch your opponent so badly out of position, you can literally hit the ball anywhere to score a point just as long as it doesn't go to the back wall.

The advantage of this wide margin of error is diminished somewhat by the difficulty beginning players have in hitting the ball out of the air. It takes more work to get in position for a volley, and it takes better timing to strike the ball on its downward path.

Verities

All three types of pass shots can be hit successfully with any one of the three basic strokes of handball (the overhand, the sidearm, and the underhand), although the time, place, and purpose of the shot almost always make one type of stroke preferable to another. For instance, to get the desired angle and spin for the two-wall pass, an openhanded, sidearm stroke is best ninety-nine percent of the time. On the other hand, a player standing near one side wall who wishes to hit a straight pass down that near wall will very often find the overhand stroke most effective in getting the ball to run own the wall without angling into it. Some situations might call for an underhand fist shot to pop the ball quickly down one of the side walls or cross court past an unsuspecting foe.

But by far the most commonly used stroke is the basic sidearm, the *sine qua non* of handball swings. This is what makes the pass so easy to hit: the simple sidearm stroke. You don't have to strain to hit the ball to the ceiling, nor do you have to bend excessively low to the floor for the kill. The ball should be struck somewhere between the knees and the waist with that smooth, sweet swing that has already made you famous on your home courts.

You don't even have to hit the ball hard. A very common error that plagues handballers of all levels is trying to hit the pass too hard. Overhitting the ball usually results in loss of control, and control is the essential factor for a well-executed straight pass or two-wall pass.

A couple of hints on control. In trying to hit the straight pass down the far wall, most players hit the front wall too low and angle the ball into the side wall too quickly. To avoid this, overplay the ball to the center of the court, hit is smoothly, and aim a little higher than you think necessary.

On the other hand, in hitting the two-all pass, most players err the other way: they hit the ball too high (sending it to the back wall), and they don't angle it enough towards the side wall (giving the opponent a fly opportunity). The remedy is to aim lower than you normally would and to risk overplaying the corner angle rather than underplaying it. This way, should you hit the ball too sharply into the corner, the ball will come out at your foe from the side wall at an acute angle and may handcuff him-it won't be an easy shot by any means.

Don't rush the pass shot. Like making all handball shots, you should wait until both you and the ball are in the correct hitting position before striking the ball. Rushing the ball means you lose control of it, tip your opponent off on the shot (instead of surprising him like you mistakenly imagine you're doing by rushing the shot), and leave yourself off balance for any return. Remember, the longer you wait, the longer your opponent must wait; and when you're on the offensive, the advantage in waiting is all yours. Winning players use the right pass shot at the right time. In deciding which pass to use, it helps immensely for you to recognize to things: whether you are on the offensive or the defensive, and the position of your opponent.

Not every pass shot is an outright attempt to score a point; in fact, very few passes should be attempted with that in mind. Many pass shots are strictly defensive shots, efforts to get out of trouble or establish a lost front court position. On these shots where you find yourself too far off balance to take a really good swing, you should simply try to get the ball around your opponent with a pass down the wall or a cross court two wall pass; you're just buying time to get yourself out of the hole into which your poor shots or your opponent's good shots have buried you. Don't try to do too much on a defensive pass shot-just play defense.

There are times, however, when you will find yourself in good position, well balanced and able to set for your shot, while your opponent is out of position, either too far forward in the front court or off to one side of the court. This is the time to go on the offensive with the pass. Try to score a point.

There's middle ground. That's when both you and your opponent have good position. When this happens, you use what is called a modified offensive pass; you hit a good, hard pass that probably won't score a point but will begin to maneuver your opponent out of position so you can score somewhere down the line in the rally. These maneuvering shots are the guts of good handball. They take hard work and patience, but they pay off with wins.

9

PEAK PERFORMANCE AND FLOW

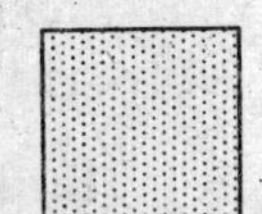

During a handball match held at a local YMCA tournament, Scot Loft-house laboured to win back the serve. The score stood 3-17. Walking heavily to the service zone, he reflected on the first game which he had lost 5-21. Lofthouse shook his head in apparent disbelief at his poor performance. Sweat dripped into his eyes. Anxiously, he waited for the referee to call the score. A glance at his opponent confirmed that he was taking his time getting ready to receive. Lofthouse risked another quick glance at the gallery. Suddenly, he loathed and feared the spectators. Their stalk-like eyes glared expectantly at him, watching intently, demanding to know what he planned to do next.

"Don't took at the spectators....never mind the sweat dripping into your eyes... Don't think about it....just play the game." Lofthouse's heart hammered erratically as he tried hard to shut his mind to distractions. He decided to call time out.

Lofthouse let the ball slip out of his hand, paused, took a long, deep breath, and exhaled slowly as if to clear his mind and body of conscious thought. He stood for a moment examining his present sensations.

Gradually the tension lines in his face dissolved. He shrugged his shoulders allowing his posture to become extremely relaxed while maintaining mental alertness. Lofthouse allowed his breathing to flow forth voluntarily from deep in his belly. With his finger he pressed in an inch or two below his navel, feeling his belly expand and contract naturally like the rthythmic ebb and flow of the ocean tides.

Lofthouse felt an inner calm come over him. He allowed his hands to open and hang easily at his sides, and noticed a heightening of awareness in all of his extremities. Tension seemed to melt, releasing an energy-like flow through his arms to the tips of antennae-like fingers.

Lofthouse bent, picked up the handball and allowed his attention to become absorbed with it. At first, he became interested in its hard, dry surface. He touched it to his cheek and found it still warm from the preceding rally. The warmth felt conforming in contrast to the cool stares of the spectators. Out of curiosity, Lofthouse put the handball to his nose and smelled it. His nostrils flared slightly. The distinct rubber door lingered for a few moments and seemed to draw his attention even deeper into the ball. He was surprised and delighted to discover these new sensations and allowed his awareness to continue its exploration. He thumbed the ball around his fingers. In previous volleys its colour appeared dull and gray with a hazy indistinct shape. Now his attention became immersed in the clearly defined round shape of the handball. It appeared to advance with a vivid, black texture. Patches of the "Ace" red label were still visible and provided a focal point for his interest.

"Time in," barked the referee exactly 30 seconds later. "The score is 3 serving 17." Lofthouse's vision was following the seam around the handball when is sense of hearing made him aware of a distinct voice calling the score automatically. Lofthouse became faintly aware of a brief intervening thought that the time out seemed to have lasted a long time, but even this reflection faded as a clear mental picture of the serve developed in his mind's eye. The image materialize into a handball rolling gently off his fingertips, falling bouncing back to the point of contact where his smooth, liquid serving stroke flowed through the ball-an artist immersed in his paint stroke.

The sound of the ball "cracking" around the walls was still echoing through the gallery as the spectators experienced a moving comeback performance. Lofthouse won the second game 21-18 and the third game 21-8. But it was not until some 15 minutes later in the searing heat of the steam room that the stale animal scent born of survival mixed with the nauseating sweat of competition to arouse Lofthouse's fatigued senses into a foggy awareness of the quality of his comeback performance. Even then, his awe was not so much for the win, but for the feeling which produced it.

Flow

This story comes to mind in view of recent research which is attempting to understand what makes up the quality of experience in which the player becomes completely immersed in an activity. In sports the experience refers to a feeling of "being on" and generally results in the player realizing a peak performance. Artists, mechanics and athletes alike have reported a general feeling that mind, body, and spirit merge into a "flow" to produce a quality performance. The person who "drops into flow" experiences an intense centering of attention and heightened awareness. His sense of time is lost and external distractions fade. Concentration does not appear to improve by "trying harder" but seems to became absorbed in an event as naturally as a child's attention becomes immersed in playing a new game. A friend once told me that he "flowed" through each page of a new issue of handball magazine.

Play and more serious matters

If we examine the qualities of handball, we discover that basically like play, they are non-practical in nature and ask us to divorce ourselves from practical matters such as work in order to enjoy them. As children, we were absorbed and delighted by the elements of play. We were not concerned with the function or outcome of play when encountered but enjoyed play as a quality of experience unique and marvellous in its own right. Our attitudes, skills, and potential were not fixed but were constantly developing, flowing forth and every moment of life was an adventure.

Michael Novak seems to have captured the spirit of play in his book the joy of sports. He writes, "Sports are not merely entertainment. But are rooted in the necessities and the aspirations of the human spirit. They should be treated with all the intelligence, care, and love the human spirit can bring to bear." In an age of professional and technical emphasis, it is difficult to imagine handball or any sport as an end in itself rather than as a means to an end. But the true handball enthusiast novice and professional would do well to recapture some of the flowing adventure provoked by his earlier child-like immersion in play.

Peak performance and flow

What are some of the elements which make up the flow experience? Generally, there is a sense of being lost in the action. It is total absorption in the game which couples the player for eight points in a row before the feeling is disrupted.

A handball player describes the feeling. "Your energy is flowing smoothly and shot execution feels liquid. You frequently lose track of the score. The body feels relaxed art the mind is alert. Sometimes the ball appears to be larger and moving slower than normal. Anticipation and execution of shots becomes as automatic as shifting gears while driving. You seem to float around the corner. There is no reflection on the other player or spectators when locked into flow. Thinking seems to block the feeling of flow."

The limitations of the printed or spoken word in fully describing the flow experience must be accepted as the natural inability of one medium to replace another. Most of us have felt the frustration which accompanies our attempt to describe a moving experience in handball to a friend. We are soon convinced that the only description lies in the experience itself.

The art of Handball

An understanding of the flow experience may be further enhanced through an appreciation of art and handball. The spontaneous nature of flow is evident is LeRoy Neiman's painting of Jimmy Jacobs. The painting flows with colour and energized motion for those who have had the pleasure of studying it. One can feel the elements of anticipation and execution flowing into place as Jacobs sets up to stroke the ball. Neiman's fluid strokes capture the flow experience by blending mood, tempo, and style, to surface the true meaning of handball. Neiman's own comment: "By venturing into and penetrating the painting the spectator discovers for himself new substances and has a prolonged contact. In similar manner. Players who lock into flow compel the spectator to become part of the experience. This is medium is the message." Everything merges in the flow experience-the handball, players, and viewers.

Flow is linked to your senses

Not all handball games will yield a deep, flow experience for the participants. Whether flow happens at all, and how deep the experience is, depends on the individual. Some seemingly gifted handball players possess what appears to be an inherent responsiveness to their senses which many increase the frequency and intensity of their flow experiences. These are players who continue to pay attention to the sensations in their bodies as they did during their childhood growth and they continue to learn, change and develop throughout their game. For most of us, however, increasing the spontaneous occurrence of flow has to be tied into some method of search and discovery which requires more than the casual use of our senses and capacity for introspection. This is true because our senses have lain dormant, underdeveloped by passive acceptance of comfortable standards, in efficient habits and mellowed attitudes.

Beyond the surface things

The newcomer to handball may ask if there is any genuinely reliable method to guide him or her in learning efficient and effective skills. A survey of various handball instruction books and observation of highly skilled players will confirm that techniques and emphases vary and change. Generally accepted teaching techniques never fail to be deceptively complex in their application to individual players. It appears that the more systematic objective, and essential substance which facilities learning. The novice, lacking in experience, has no other course than to let his senses provide the necessary feedback to develop his game.

Sensory awareness is a means to finer muscular control as well as increased flow opportunities because the players senses, perceptions and action become totally immersed in the game. The following suggestions and exercises are not meant to be "How-to-do-it" instructions. They contain no rules formulas or guarantees. The exercises are meant to be sensed and understood through experience for the purpose of experienced singly is of any significance, but each sensation represents a part of what eventually occurs in the total flow experience.

See the ball. Easy to say but difficult to does we have all learned. Habitually, we have learned to rely largely on our sense of sight to "watch the ball." This reminder generally focuses our attention on the obvious shape of the handball. The boundary or continuous edge of the handball, which stands out from the space and walls around it, give if the round shape we perceive. But even the round shape can appear soft and hazy, or sharp and distinct depending on how near or distant the ball is. For the handball player to expand his sense of sight he may find it helpful to look beyond the obvious round shape of the ball.

According to fundamental principles of art, contrasting and bright colours provide a focal point of interest and are associated with foreground or near positions. Concentration may be improved by allowing your eyes to focus, not only on a round black ball, but on the contrasting red. "Ace" label as you prepare to serve See if you can focus your sight on the red label as the ball rotates through space during a volley. If your budget is like mine, you probably use the same ball for three months! In this case, either periodically paint your own label on the ball or forget this exercise. However, the argument for having a bright or multicoloured ball with distinct seams would appear to be supported on the basis of facilitating the player's concentration as well as spectator considerations.

Another exercise which may help the player extend his sight of the ball is to visualize the line or path represented by the ball as it bounces around the court. It represents a path of action which links the player's stokes. The line moves and lives in the present, pulsating with emotions and conveying feelings, strategies and intentions. In this sense, the ball's trajectory may appear as smooth and flowing. Or as tense and erratic as the players themselves. The ball's abrupt and unexpected changes of direction create angular lines which our eyes find exciting and full of challenging interest. Watching the ball in this manner becomes visually entertaining and stimulating.

As the player practices following the trajectory of the ball, his senses may give him the feeling that he is "riding with the ball" as it moves from one point of contact to another. Riding the ball becomes a self-renewing circuit which continually draws our attention deeper into the volley until it is ended. Concentration appears to be facilitated because the changes for spontaneous flow to occur.

Visual attention is but sense which contributes to our total perception of the handball. Expanding sensory awareness requires the critical probing of the ball and ourselves with as many senses as possible.

Feel the ball. Generally, smooth, light and easy feelings accompany well performed strokes because these sensations yield greater sensitivity and finer muscular action. Excess tension and superfluous effort cause the body to draw itself together in defense, and prevent it from organizing itself properly for action. The tense player hinders himself to flow and improved performance as surely as an intentional hider prevents him from executing a full, uninhibited stroke.

For example, some players are so hung up on winning every game to maintain their status in the local club pecking order, they will not allow themselves to relax and feel their strengths and weaknesses. They may lack self-confidence in their non-dominant side and adopt the "trying hard" style as an indicator of their will to win. Generally, these players will not relax because they feel to be relaxed is to be weak. Instead, they remain in a state of constant tension and execute stiff, robot-like strokes. Most of us have seen the type of driver who grips the steering wheel tightly and leans forward with his face set in a light mask of concentration. Likewise, tenses facial strains and muscular tightness give the handball player the feeling and appearance of "redness" and "trying hard" but actually hider the flow of sensory feedback necessary for improved performance.

With this idea in mind, allow your attention to focus on what it feels like to stroke the ball during warm-ups, practice, or even a game. You may have to give up a few points in order to notice the sensations generated when your hand meets the ball at point of contact, but awareness of this feeling is a means to increased accuracy. Can you distinguish the difference in feeling when the ball is contacted at the base of your fingers as opposed to your palm? Does the ball feel like it is rolling off your fingertips or does it feel like a collision at point of impact? Stroke the ball ten times both sides and allow yourself to experience how it feels to stroke the ball. See if you can describe the quality of vibrations which are sent up your arms and through your body. Compare the subtle differences of these feelings with both right and left sides.

These feelings are experienced through the sense of touch but are interpreted in the mind. Awareness of these feelings is a means to finer muscular control, as well as increased flow opportunities. Because the mind and body are so completely absorbed with interpreting these feelings, it is less likely to be distracted by external events such as spectators opponent's gestures or thoughts about winning or losing. The total immersion of our mind and body yields a feeling of continued flow similar to the merging "steady state" a child's top achieves as it follows faster in the same direction. Our only concern should be with keeping the flow going. When thoughts of the next point or winning the game enter the mind, the flow is disrupted as surely as an outside force acting on the top causes it to lose its stability.

Hear the ball. Discover the immediate effects of listening to the sound of the ball at its point of impact with your hand. Try to correlate this sound with the feelings you experienced in the previous exercise. While it is not probable that you can listen to the sound the ball makes upon contact with your hand and also be consciously aware of what it feels like on the same stroke, you can experience the different sensations singly through practice. Your mind and body will store these sensations in the subconscious. Later, as you expand sensory awareness, the composite of these sensations will surface for use in directing future strokes with little or no conscious effort at all.

Serve the ball and listen to the sound it makes at point of contact. Is the sound a soft click or a dull thud? Do your most effective serves sound the same as less effective ones? Was the served ball that seemed to "crack" off the front wall executed with a smooth fluid serving stroke? Stroke the ball with the dominant side and listen to what the ball "has to say". Compare these sensations with the non-dominant side. This kind of sensory awareness must be kept fresh by constant practice. Happily, the opportunities for this practice are present every day at your local club or YMCA. You have only to break the chains of past habits.

Smell the ball. Well yes, we think it does make sense. Pun intended. The handball does have a distinct rubber. Go ahead place the ball to your nose odor immediately. You may even be surprised to discover that the smell lingers in your awareness and absorbs your attention for a few moments, or you may be asking yourself what all this has to do with stroking the handball. Here goes.

The fine art of allowing your attention to become completely absorbed with the ball is easily disrupted. Because we have aspirations, we can just as easily allow our attention to linger on thoughts of further goals such as winning the game. Likewise, we have a tendency to reflect on past experiences such as the last point we blew. Such thoughts usually enter our mind as we begin to serve, and we know full well they contribute nothing to executing the present task at hand. Such thoughts only interfere with the flow of present sensory perceptions and actions necessary to stroke that elusive little ball. Thus when we have difficulty centering our attention on the ball, we might purposely place the handball to our nose. The distinct rubber odor should not fail to penetrate our minds and collect wandering thoughts for the moments we need to focus our attention on the ball until it is served.

Taste the ball. Foul, play....wait.....no fair..... hinder .....check the ball! No doubt distinct of a handball would capture our attention not to mention the wonderful reverse hops a wet handball would impact. But we must kiss the sense of taste goodbye-a rule is a rule.

Our senses are continually bringing in information on which we base our perceptions and actions in order to play handball. Our concern is with expanding sensory awareness so that our perceptions and actions related to handball will be more flowing and accurate. The spontaneous flow feeling we sometimes experience involves the harmonious merging of our sensations, perceptions, and the game. It appears that the player who probes and extends his sensory awareness through constant practice may be able to increase the occurrence and intensity of flow. That the player is able to realize improved performance near the outer limits of his skills almost seems secondary to capturing the true nature of the handball experience-flow.

10

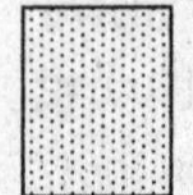

PRINCIPLES APPLIED TO HANDBALL

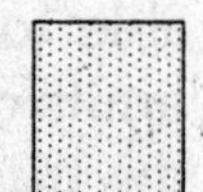

Every handballer has an innate desire to improve his game as rapidly as possible, but a limited amount of time he can justify spending in this pursuit. Motor learning is a branch of experimental psychology that deals exclusively with the learning of physical or motor skills. The learning principles that follow have been specifically related to the efficient learning and teaching of handball drills, but could be applied to almost any physical skill. For the reader to appreciate this article, there must be an understanding of the distinction made between the concepts of learning and performance.

A psychology measures performance changes. Let us assume we have a beginning handballer who diligently practices back wall kill shots every day for 25 days. Every fifth day he measures his performance by determining the percentage of 50 shots he is able to kill, and records this score as point on the vertical axis of the graph. Bay connecting these performance measures (points) with a line. He has plotted a classical motor learning curve. The change between day 5 and day 25 is the inferred amount of learning that has occurred. In this example the handballer improved approximately 20% in kill shot accuracy over 20 days. Of the learning principles that should be utilized, the first and foremost principles is what a learning psychologist would refer to as a response trial, or in layman's language, practice. The more you practice a particular motor skill the higher the acquisition level. The classical research paper on extended practice was written by Grossman who tested industrial workers over a three year period with millions and responses and found learning was still occurring. In essence there is no substitute for practice in the learning of a motor skill. Any top athlete will attest to the fact that it takes long, hard hours of practice to achieve championship performance. With the necessity for practice established, learning principles derived from other areas of motor learning will be introduced to enable him to efficiently utilize his practice time.

This brings us to a concept known as feedback one of the strongest and most important variables controlling performance and learning. When a motor movement is made, you receive a wealth of sensory feedback from various sense organs regarding that movement. You may also receive feedback from a coach instructor, or by watching a video tape replay. The practising handballer should attempt to optimise all sources of feedback that are available to him. To utilize feedback effectively one needs to from a model (visual image in the mind) of the correct way to execute a given shot. Next, hit the selected shot, receive feedback from the aforementioned sources and use the feedback to compare the shot to the model (error measurement). Then make a cognitive decision as to how to reduce the error or variation from the model; hit the shot again and repeat this process until the error is essentially eliminated. Ask a club pro to provide the correct model for basic shots that can be practised alone. It is more efficient to learn a skill correctly in the beginning thus avoiding the need to break a well-learned bad habit at a later date. A video tape recorder aids the club pro in spotting and pointing out fine details with fast movements and enables him to see,, rather than having someone describe, how you look in action. Another excellent source of feedback that aspiring players should utilize are the top players in the club. Ask any of these players to observe your play and offer suggestions for improving your game. You will undoubtedly receive a multitude of suggestions and personal opinions which can only add to your overall knowledge of the game.

Feedback leads us to an area in motor learning known as social facilitation, which examines the effect of people upon people. Research strongly suggests that the presence of other persons during the early stages of learning has a detrimental effect upon skill acquisition. The literature also indicated that, once a skill is well-learned, the presence of other persons tends to elicit peak performance. A rather detailed theoretical explanation has been formulated to explain these results. Therefore, the literature suggests you practice alone or with just an instructor present. Once you have acquired a high skill level, play on an exhibition court where people are watching as this should get you up for a top performance. If you are trying to learn a few shot go back to the secluded court to practice.

The next area of interest is concerned with the effect of "fatigue" on learning. To eliminate debate as to a suitable definition of fatigue let us assume you have just played a vigorous hour-long match and are tired. Most players assume that if they are in a fatigued or tired state they cannot learn anything and practice would be futile. On the contrary, several researchers have indicated that fatigue is a performance variable rather than a learning variable. Your practice performance level while in a fatigued state will be depressed, but when you return to a rested state your performance level will increase to the same level it would have reached if you had practised for an equivalent amount of time while in a rested state. During a vigorous match you receive a wealth of sensory feedback and should become aware of those aspects of your game which could use improvement. Practice before these invaluable feedback traces are forgotten. Practising while in a fatigued state may also increase your endurance for your next match. Remember that even though your practice performance is sub par, learning is still occurring and will manifest itself when you return to a rested state.

We will now concern ourselves with some of the mental aspects of learning a motor skill. Any champion athlete will attest to the fact that it takes tremendous mental concentration to elicit peak physical performance. Research reviews have shown that mental practice of motor skill improves acquisition or learning of that motor skill. Mental practice is generally defined as cognitive rehearsal of a skill with no overt physical movement. To use mental practice effectively, you should find a quiet location, close your eyes and try to visualize yourself repeated hitting a specific shot, concentrating on all the factors you would if you were actually hitting the shot. The importance of mental concentration cannot be over-emphasized if this techniques to be effectively utilized. Several practice periods of 2 or 3 minutes each, with a short rest period, should aid skill acquisition. Mental practice could be utilized as a warm-up technique and has the advantage of enabling one to practice while injured or unable to obtain court time. The server in handball could use mental practice in the 10 seconds he has to initiate play. Many players fail to concentrate during the serve and seem to just put the ball in play. This nullifies the advantage they had in the serving position.

Next we shall concern ourselves with the area in motor learning known as retention. Maximising retention of well-learned motor skills should also be of interest to the avid handballer. If you have spent the hours of practice necessary to learn a skill, you certainly wish to maintain this high level of proficiency. Research literature shows that motor skills are well retained over time. The research has shown that after a long period of inactivity, it takes less practice to relearn a skill to a given level than it required to reach that level initially. You should spend an hour or two per week, in addition to playing practising all the basic shots to make these well-learned skills resistant to forgetting.

A second area of research dealing with retention is called short-term motor memory and has practical applications for learning handball skills. The research indicates we have short-term and long-term motor memory stores. The short-term store lasts from approximately five seconds to two minutes and measurable forgetting can occur during this short time interval. To utilize a skill or shot in a game situation effectively, the skill must be transferred from your short-to long-term memory store. Since forgetting has been shown to occur in just a few seconds, you should practice one specific shot at a time for at least fifty to one hundred trials, as opposed to hitting a few ceiling balls, a few shots righthanded, and a few shots lefthanded, etc. Using the latter method you may forget a shot before you have learned it. Use several balls while practising to avoid spending time retrieving balls. Follow the advice of the top pros who recommend long periods of practice on specific shots. Once a skill is ingrained in your short-term memory store, it will gradually transfer into your long-term motor memory store.

Of course motivation is necessary for one to spend the hours of practice required for top level play. When a new skill is being learned, the rate of learning is comparatively fast. This rapid improvement is easy to recognize and acts as a motivation for the practising player. As any handballer continues to improve he reaches a point of diminishing returns where a great amount of practice is required for a noticeable skill differential separates many top club players from the pros. A player may utilize several techniques to maintain his motivation to practice. Set up a definite monthly practice schedule which lists the shots and amount of time you feel you should spend on various aspects of your game. Test yourself weekly by setting up an arbitrary scoring system and plot your results in the from of a learning curve.

For example, place a box in a back corner of the court and court the number of ceiling shots out of 50 that hit the box. Practice various times during the day and vary the length of your practice sessions as repetition leads to boredom. Practice with various people on specific aspects of the game that require a partner, such as serving and the return of serve. One person may work on specific serves while his partner works on service returns. Finally, don't be discouraged if you are just beginning the game and other new players seem to posses superior skills. Researchers have shown that initial performance levels of individuals are insignificant after extended periods of practice. Stick with it. By utilizing efficient practice techniques you may surpass many players you had previously considered unbeatable.

This leads to an interesting phenomenon known as bilateral transfer which is applicable to handball due to the ambidextrous nature of the game. Researches have shown that a skill learned with one hand transfers to the opposite limb. If you learn a shot with one hand a position of this skill should transfer to your opposite hand. If one hand or limb is injured, practising with the opposite hand should reduce any retention losses in the injured due to the forced inactivity.

A final area in motor learning known as warm-up has been given considerable attention by physiologists. They have pointed out that you should stretch and warm-up your muscles to improve flexibility contraction velocity, and reduce the probability of muscle stiffness and injury. Viewing warm-up from a psychological perspective researches have observed that on motor tasks where injury is not a factor, a warm-up period will result in improved performance. Apparently one must acquire the right mental set before top performance can be elicited. The literature suggests a warm-up period of at least ten minutes during which you practice all the shots you might utilize in a pending match. This should follow your general physiological warm-up of stretching and jogging to improve flexibility and heat up the muscles for your match. Utilization of these experimentally derived motor learning principles should lead to efficient and rapid handball skill acquisition.

BEHAVIOURAL ANALYSIS

The role of psychology in sports has enjoyed increased popularity in the past few years. Both professional and amateur athletes in many sports stress the importance of using psychology during competition. During a match an athlete may "psych out" his opponent, develop a cerebral "flow" or "psych himself up" In many cases when the contest is close and the opponents are evenly matched, it is suggested that the use of psychology is the major factor which determines who wins and who loses.

Most investigators who have studied the psychology of sports have used the verbal report of highly skilled athletes as their main source of information. These verbal reports usually describe the sensations and feelings which existed during certain periods of the game or match. The reports are then analysed in an attempt to understand what makes a winner. The method of examining these reported sensations in order to gain insight into psychological factors is known as the clinical method. Clinical researches also use psychological tests, both written and oral, to gain additional information regarding an individual's personality. Going even further, several clinical psychologists have attempted to correlate personality "types" with success in specific sports.

The clinical approach has gathered valuable information regarding clusters of personality traits which correlate with success in competition; however the clinical method fails to provide any information which will allow predictions to be made of the future performance of a specific individuals. In many cases an athlete will excel in a sport even though his personality inventory or profile suggests other-wise. Also, findings obtained from psychological tests do not indicate which factors in an individual's environment are important for the development of particular skills. For example, how to various training procedures in handball affect later on-the-court performance? Does the self-taught handball player do as well as one who receives professional instruction? If professional instruction does produce more proficient handball players, when is the training most effective-at the in novice level or after playing several years? If there do exist differences long term performance on the handball court which reflect varying methods of instruction how can one best exploit the most effective teaching procedure?

These kinds of questions have resulted in the development of another method of studying the psychology of sports. This approach known as applied experimental psychology, makes use of the observable behaviour of an individual rather than verbal reports as the measure of psychological events. Instead of asking a handball player how the felt after making a dramatic backcourt kill shot, the experimental psychologist simply records the kill shot as an event which occurred during the progress of the match. The main interest of the experimental psychologist is the development of procedures which increase on the court behaviours such as kill shots, passing shots well placed ceiling shots, or drop shots and reduce unwanted behaviours which result in errors on the court.

The reason for the interest in the development of such procedures in sports is based on evidence obtained from nonsport areas which have demonstrated repeatedly that skills are acquired faster developed or altered with less trouble and maintained for longer periods of time when certain training procedures are used. The main reason for the success of experimental psychology is its use of settings where the behaviours has an advantage over verbal reports because changes in observable behaviour can be measured and controlled. The study of the acquisition of highly refined motor skills such as flying an aircraft, driving an automobile, or performing industrial work, indicates the changes in reaction time, information processing (stimulus discrimination) and the force of a response can be altered through changes in the parameters of the training procedure.

In much the same way that an airplane pilot's reaction speed can be increased by training him to become knowledgeable of practicable changes in his environment, a handball player can also be trained to respond to the direction and speed of a handball coming off the front or side wall, thereby increasing the amount of time available to make a decision concerning the most effective return shot. Information processing, which is another way to asking what to do with the ball once you are in position to stroke it can be improved by a training program which stresses the relationship between specific responses and their probability of success. Based on the findings obtained with short amount of time to play the game using strategies which usually take months of court competition to a acquire. One of the most beneficial effects of the applied behavioural method of instruction is the speed in which tasks are learned. It is not inconceivable that proper training techniques can reduce the amount of practice time required to become proficient in playing handball by fifty percent.

One example of instructing handball with an experimentally based methodology is a step-by-step program in which players are trained to become more proficient in playing handball. This method of teaching handball differs from the typical program in a variety of ways. First, the player learns specific tasks, such as the passing shot, kill shot, and various serves, as discrete items. Instead of beginning training by the student simply walking onto the court and starting to knock the ball around, the player is required to practice each task separately until he can demonstrate that his skill is at a level designated by the instructor. The individual's performance requirement for each task which is known as the criterion level, is gradually altered throughout the training program.

Initially, response requirements for successful shots are quite low and can be performed easily; only as the individuals skills increase does the criterion level requirement become more difficult. Second each player is required to demonstrate proficiency in each task before being allowed to play handball competitively. By doing this the individual learns all basic shots equally well and thereby avoids weak spots in his game prior to the beginning of actual competition. By having a well-balanced armament of responses prior to competitive play, the novice will not depended on one or two "favourite" shots. Finally the teacher makes use of players bracket which can be entered only after a specific level of handball playing skill has been demonstrated. It has been shown that the entrance into the players bracket will function as a reward (reinforcer) and will enhance learning speed.

While specific procedures which can be employed to train handball players have not been detailed in this articles, it should be stressed that the methods involved are fundamentally different from those typically used to teach handball. Perhaps the most important point is that the progress of each player is continually monitored so skill requirements can be tailored to the individual. By altering requirements based upon the individual's change in handball proficiency, one can assure that the player will enjoy a history of success from the very first time he picks up a handball. It is well-known fact that racquet-ball has enjoyed an increase in participation due to the ease with which the skills required to play the game are acquired. Individuals who begin playing racquetball usually have more initial success at the game than those players who start playing handball. Thus, many people choose racquetball over handball simply because it is easier to learn the experimental method of teaching handball can increase the amount of success the novice handball player will derive and in doing so ensure that the student will continue to participate in the sport. It is the ability to engineer a history of success into the training program which makes the applied experimental method so effective as a teaching device.

The use of an applied behaviour analysis of sports in the United States is currently in its infant stage. Based upon the extent to which applied psychology has been demonstrated to be effective in developing skills in other areas, however, the benefits derived from a systematic teaching method based upon experimentally verifiable findings, would be substantial. Once the technology is completely developed and put into use it is certain the methods of instruction used in applied experimental psychology will be powerful tool from which coaches of many sports, including handball will be able to benefit.

12 SUCCESSFUL HANDBALL PLAYER

In any competitive endeavour a few individuals experience unusual success and rise to the from within their group of peers. This success is attributed to several factors, not the least of which is hard work and dedication to the job or activity. For an individual in sports to excel to where he is recognized as an accomplished athlete takes more than mere dedication. Dedication will allow a person to develop to his own maximum potential in that sport, but will not automatically insure the success of a champion.

The question can be asked "what are the attributes or the characteristics of those individuals who have excelled over other players and have experienced unusual success in handball? "Physically, they have developed themselves to a very high level of conditioning. Their cardiovascular systems, which includes the heart, lungs and circulatory system, have the efficiency to allow long periods of sustained intense activity.

Also, the muscles of the body have been developed to the point where there is sufficient strength to move in the court and execute all the shots.

The muscles must have the endurance to perform in lengthy matches or even lengthy tournaments without appreciable fatigue or substantial muscle that could interfere with effective playing.

The third attribute would be neuromuscular coordination. Strong muscles and an efficient cardiovascular do not insure skill. Proper technique of all the essential shots must be perfected. A player's mind cannot be focused on such fundamentals as the proper way to hit the ball during the heat of a match, but execution of the shot must be a coordinated reflex action, learned by many hours of practice and play in previous matches.

These three factors-cardiovascular endurance strength and neuromuscular coordination—are each vital for competitive success. However, these purely physical traits are not the only factors that are characteristic of success. If they were, handball success could be predicated on the basis of a physical fitness test.

Competition in sports also involves mental or psychological factors. It is difficult to assess a person's inner drive to win. And, certainly, there is varied drive from game-to or match-to-match. No athlete can remain at an emotional peak at all times during a game or match.

Each person, however functions from within a certain personally framework unique to himself. An individual's personality profile has been developed from past experiences with family and environment and also from his own internally developed ideas. This psychological framework is not rigid, where a person becomes totally predictable nor is it ever-changing, where a person's personality would be constantly changing. Investigations have been conducted studying the profiles of certain groups in order to determine if and how they differed from other groups or the population in general. For example, Olympic athletes have been found to demonstrate higher degrees of emotional maturity, calmness, and constancy in interests. These Olympic athletes are also more assertive, independent, headstrong and admiration-demanding than the general population. Other personality characteristics which appear to distinguish these athletes from the "norm" are that they tend to be adventurous impulsive, and have a carefree outlook on life. In another personality dimension, the Olympic champions appear to manifest a higher degree of self-confidence, cheerfulness and, as a rule, a lesser sense of inadequacy than the general population. College football players have also been compared to the average college population. In general, the results indicate that this type of athlete is more action-oriented, dominant, group-dependent, self-reliant, and "down-to-earth" than the typical college age adult.

The psychological inventory that is used in many investigations of personality characteristics is one called Cattell's Sixteen Personality Factor (16PF). This inventory measures sixteen different identifiable traits based on the results of a written examination. Each of the traits is set up on a continuum where the extreme opposite characteristics are on each end of the scale and a normal range is in the center. As an example, in studying one of the traits, allow score would be indicate shyness, restraint, and timidness while a high score would be indicative of someone who is adventuresome, bold, and uninvited. Invitations to participate in this type of psychological inventory were extended to 32 of the nation's best handball players. There were 19 who completed the examination and the results are summarized in this report. Their responses to the examination were evaluated by the student Counselling Services Testing Service of the University of Illinois at Chicago Circle.

On the basis of the test results, it is apparent that these handball players differed considerably from the general population on two of the 16 traits. Also, on two other traits the scores were consistent enough to indicate tendencies away from the population average. Of the remaining 12 traits, the inventory scores indicated the players scored within the normal range. One of the too traits in which there was a marked difference between the players and the general population is that describing the players as being very forth-right, natural and unpretentious as opposed to shrewd calculating and worldly. The scores of the players on this trait indicated that, as a group they tended to be gregarious had simple tastes, and were genuinely emotionally expressive. If one were to characterize how the typical handball player interacted socially with others from this psychological trait, he or she might use descriptive terms such as "Completely direct" and "spontaneously outspoken". Thus, the typical handball player is more likely to be honest, open and direct attitude when they interact with him. Compared to Olympic athletes handball players are more unpretentious, open and friendly.

The second of the two traits where a significant difference occurred between handball players and the public at large was one indicating the players were abstract thinkers-a trait usually associated with more intelligent and bright persons-as opposed to concrete thinkers, associated with less intelligence. As a group, the handball players appear to be quite similar to Olympic athletes in this personality dimension. Both groups tend to be more persevering, fast-learning and adaptable to changing events and times than the general adult population. This is probably the result of a higher level of education by the handball players and Olympic athletes. In fact, the scores indicated the group average was near the 90th percentile of the continuum, a very high rating.

Of the other two traits where moderately strong tendencies were revealed, the players tended to be more expedient about matters, disregarding rules and feeling few obligations as opposed to being conscientious and moralistic. Interpretation of this psychological tendency is aided by the fact that Olympic athletes are wire similar to the handball players on this trait. Perhaps this indicates those in the population who are the "best" at what they do have to be expedient and disregard rules and normal. In other words, in order to become the "best" a person has to different and not do "what is expected."

The second characteristic shows that the handball players tend to be self-sufficient, preferring their own decision making, and being resourceful to group dependency and being a "joiner." This finding seems logical since handball players are individual competitors and they must rely on their own talents and abilities as compared to members of a team.

The results of the scoring of one more trait also

deserves mentioning, not for the group average that was attained, but rather for the variability of the individual scores. On this factor, extremely low scores indicate the subjects are humble, mild, and accommodating, while the opposite would indicate assertive, aggressive, and stubborn behaviours patterns. It would appear that although the group average of handball players was close to that of the general population, handball players fall at both extremes of the personality dimension. Some players are very easy-going considerate, and humble, while others are very assertive and aggressive.

There have been certain characteristics found that these highly skills handball players have in common. This is not to say, however, that each player of championship calibre is just like the other, but rather they tend to have similarities in their personalities. Because of their dedication to the game and the success they have had, one would expect their personalities to be different from the normal population, and as a group to have certain similarities.

The results of this study indicate that the highly skilled handball player tends to:

(1) be bright and intelligent,

(2) be quite open, natural and unpretentious,

(3) be self-sufficient and prefer to live by his own decisions,

(4) feel few obligations,

(5) deal with his problems as expediently as possible.

This investigation does not answer the question, "Does a person need this kind of profile in order to excel at the game of handball?" Or, "Does this type of profile evolve as a result of success in a sport?" Or, to put it another way, "Are champions born or are they made?" It is the authors contention that an individual is not likely to achieve great success in handball unless he is a self-motivated individual possessing the traits identified in this investigation. These traits are a necessary ingredient and are important as the physical aspect of the game. It is still a debatable question but at least we have gained some insight into the personality of the handball player at the point in time when he is a highly successful player.

13

THE CHAMPIONS

The best player in the country for one full year until the next national tournament rolls around, a champion. It's a title full of meaning, rich in tradition, a crown many a young handball player has dreamed of, spent hours practising for, but achieved by only a few.

Some won through consummate skill, some through backbreaking work, some through masterful thinking. Some champions overcome unbelievable barriers to win; some found good fortune smoothed the court against opponents who desired the national title every bit as much as they.

The champions were (are) men like the rest of us. From all walks of like, with all manner of personalities, of many different talents, they are distinguished by nothing more than this accident of fate, that they won a national crown. Does that mean we should honour them the less? Certainly not.

As handball players, they are our ideals. The champions deserve our respect for several reasons.

Winners conquer fear. Jim Jacobs won six national crowns, every one of them a triumph over fear: "When it came time to go to the courts for the national finals match, this match we had worked months and years to play in, we wanted to go the opposite direction from the courts. The intense apprehension I felt never left me until forced myself in the court and the match began."

Championship courage conquered extreme leg circulation problems, Knee surgery, the loss of an infant daughter. Three straight years of final match defeats; twisted ankles, broken fingers, bleeding heads mean nothing to the champion except one more minor hurdle to overcome.

The champions inspire us to greater action, to dedication and courage we alone could not muster ourselves, but because those who have gone before us have done it, we find some hidden reserve of strength to do it also.

The records of the champions will live on; they will be broken and superseded. But we'll remember them for the heights they reached and the examples they set.

In the first official national tournament, Bill "Murder Ball" Ranft defeated Joe Lacey for the title, 21-13, 21-11. The tournament was held at the Los Angeles Athletic Club with 13 players competing most going both ways (singles and doubles). In fact, Ranft teamed with Lacey to win the doubles title.

Ranft learned his handball at Golden Gate Park in San Francisco represented the Olympic Club for a time, and then moved to Los Angeles Athletic Club in water polo, basketball, and track in addition to his excellent play on the handball courts.

He was a champion who gave back to the game. He tutored many young players, formed the Harold

Lloyd Handball Club at MR. Llyod's spacious estate in Beverly Hills, and even after his playing days were over he kept current on the sport and its development.

The game was a little bit different in Bill's day. Two shorts were permitted, the third being a handout. Ceiling, back wall, and three wall serves were permitted. A hinder was allowed only if the ball did not reach the front wall, and body contact was generally overlooked.

Despite the roughness of the game, Ranft seemed to have been a popular player. Carroll Van Court, handball instructor at the LAAC describes "Murder Ball" as, "a very popular player because he never stalls, never always plays a fair, clean, hard, brilliant game, and gives the best he has." Bill Ranft knew the game from soup to cigars and back again. He was as much at home in the handball court as a pickpocket in a crowed. He maintained a relationship with the game of handball all his life, which was 81 years long.

14

RULES AND REGULATIONS

THE PLAYING COURT

The playing court is a 40 meters long and 30 meters wide rectangle, consisting of two goal areas and a playing area. The longer boundary lines are called side lines, and the shorter ones are referred to as a goal lines (between the goal posts) or "outer goal lines" (on either side of the goal).

The condition of the playing court must not be altered in such a way that one team gains an advantage. A goal is placed in the centre of each goal line. The goals must be firmly attached to the floor. They have an interior height of 2 meters and a width of 3 meters. The goalposts are joined by a horizontal crossbar. The rear side of the goalposts shall be in line with the rear edge of the goal line. The goalposts and the crossbar must have a 8 cm square cross section and consist of a uniform material (e.g., wood, light metal, or synthetic material). They must be painted on all sides in bands of two contrasting colours which also contrast clearly with the background.

The goalposts and the crossbar shall be painted in the same colour where they join. This colour shall extend for 28 cm in each direction. All other rectangles of colour shall be 20 cm long. The goals must have a net, attached in such a way that a ball thrown into the goal cannot immediately rebound out of it.

The goal area is defined by the goal-area line, which is drawn as follows: (i) a 3 meters long line in front of the goal, parallel to, and 6 meters away from, the goal line; and (ii) quartercircles joining its ends to the goal line, each with a radius of 6 meters measured from the rear inner corner of the goalposts. The free-throw line (9-meter line) is a broken line, where both the segments and the spaces between them measure 15 cm. The line is drawn 3 meters outside, and parallel to, the goal-area line.

The 7-meter line is 1 meter long. It is parallel to, and 7 meters away from the rear edge of, the goal line, right in front f the goal. The goalkeeper's restraining line (the 4-meter line) is 15 cm long. It is parallel to, and 4 meters away from the rear edge of, the goal line, right in front of the goal.

The centre line connects the midpoints of the two side lines. Each of the two substitution lines is limited at a distance of 4.5 meters from the center line by a line which is parallel to the center line and extends 15 cm into the court.

As guidance to the teams, these lines also extend 15 cm outside the court. All lines on the court are part of the area which they enclose. They shall be 5 cm wide (except as in 1:10) and shall always be clearly visible. 1:10 The goal lines shall be 8 cm wide between the goalposts, so that they match the width of the posts.

The Playing time

The playing time for all male and female teams with

players of age 18 and above is 2 halves of 30 minutes with a half-time break of 10 minutes.

The playing time begins with the court referee's whistle for the initial throw-off. It ends with the automatic final signal from the public clock or the final signal from the timekeeper.

Infractions and unsportsmanlike conduct which take place before the final signal are to be punished, also if this cannot be done until after the signal. The court referee ends the game only after the necessary free-throw or 7-meter throw has been taken and its result has been established. An infraction during the execution for such free-throw cannot, however, lead to a free-throw in the opposite direction. The reams change ends for the second half of the game.

The referees decide if an when the playing time is to be interrupted and when it is to be restarted. They give the timekeeper the signal when the playing time is to be interrupted (time-out) and restarted.

Interruption of playing time is to be indicated to the timekeeper through three short blasts on the whistle and the sign. The whistle must always be blown to indicate the restart of the game after a time-out (1 6-.3a). The throw must be retaken, if the final signal sounds when a free throw or a 7-meter throw is being executed or when the ball is already in the air. The immediate result of the retaken throw is to be established before the referees end the game.

Infractions or unsportsmanlike conduct which take place during the execution of such a free-throw or a 7-meter throw must be punished.

If the referees determine that the timekeeper has given the final signal too early, they must keep the players on the court and play the remaining time. The team which was in possession of the ball at the time of the premature signal will remain in possession when the game resumes.

If the first half of a game has been terminated too late, the second half must be shortened accordingly. Overtime is played, following a 5-minute intermission, if a game is tied at the end of the normal playing time and a winner has to be determined. A coin toss determines ball possession and the right to choose ends.

The overtime period always consists of 2 halves of 5 minutes. The teams change ends at half time but there is no half-time break. If the game is again after a first overtime period, a second period is played after a 5-minute break and coin toss. This overtime period also has 2 halves of 5 minutes. if the game is still tied, the winner will be determined in accordance with the rules for the particular competition.

THE BALL

The ball is made of leather or a synthetic material. It must be spherical. The surface must not be shiny or slippery. At the start of the game, the ball used in a men's game must have a circumference of 58-60 cm and a weight of 425-475 grams.

In a women's game, the circumference is 54-56 cm and the weight 325-400 grams. At every game, there must be two balls available that conform with the rules.

Once the game has started, the ball must not be changed unless this becomes absolutely necessary. It is obligatory to use Official IHF balls, marked with the IHF logo, in all international games.

THE TEAM

A team consists of 12 players. The players must be listed in the scoresheet.

The team must use a goalkeeper at all times. No more than 7 players (6 court players and 1 goalkeeper) may be present on the court at the same time. The remaining players are substitutes. Only the substitutes, any suspended players, and 4 team officials are allowed in the team's substitution area.

The team officials must be listed in the scoresheet and May not be replaced during the course of the game. One of them must be designated as responsible for the team. Only this official is allowed to address the timekeeper/scorekeeper and, possibly, the referees.

A team must have at least 5 players ready on the court at the start of the game. The number of players on a team can be increased up to 12, at any time during the game, including overtime. The game may continue, even if a team is reduced to less than 5 players on the court.

A player is entitled to participate if he is present at the start of the game and is included in the scoresheet. A player who is entitled to participate may, at any tin, enter the court over the team's own substitution line. Players and team officials who arrive after the game has started must obtain their entitlement to participate from the timekeeper/scorekeeper.

A player who is not entitled to participate shall be disqualified if he enters the court and the opponents shall be awarded a free-throw Substitutes may enter the game, at any time and repeatedly, without notifying the timekeeper/scorekeeper, as long as the players they are replacing have already left the court.

This also applies to the substitution of goalkeepers. The players shall always leave and enter the court over their own team's substitution line.

During a time-out, it is permitted to enter the court from the substitution area:

(i) for a normal substitution or (ii) with explicit permission from the referees.

A faulty substitution shall be penalized with a free-throw for the opponents from the place where the guilty player crossed the side line. In addition, the player shall be given a 2-minute suspension. If the faulty substitution takes place during a stoppage in the game, the player shall be suspended but the game is to be restarted in the way which corresponds to the reason for the stoppage.

In the event of a seriously unsportsmanlike conduct or an assault in connection with, or immediately following, a faulty substitution, the guilty player shall be disqualified or excluded, respectively. If an additional player enters the court. without a substitution, or if a substitute illegally interferes with the game from the substitution area, there shall be a 2-minute suspension for the player, and another player must leave the court so that the team plays with reduced strength for 2 minutes. If a player enters the court while serving a 2-minute suspension, he shall be given an additional 2-minute suspension. This suspension shall begin immediately, and another player must therefore leave the, court during the overlap between the first and the second suspension. The responsible team official must select this other player.

If he refuses then the referees will decide who must leave the court. All the court players on a team must wear identical uniforms. The combinations of colours and design for the two teams must be clearly distinguishable from each other. A player who is used as goalkeeper must wear colours which distinguish him from the court players of both teams and the goalkeeper of the opposing team.

The players shall be numbered from 1-20 the Numbers must be at least 20 cm high in the back of the shirt and at least 10 cm in the front. The colour of the numbers must contrast clearly with the colour of the uniform.

The players must wear sports shoes. It is not permitted to wear any objects that could be dangerous to players, for instance, head or face protection, bracelets, watches, rings, necklaces or chains, earrings, glasses without restraining bands or with solid frames, or any other objects which could be dangerous to the players.

Players who do not meet this requirement will not be allowed to take part until they have corrected the problem. The captain of each team must wear an armlet around the upper arm. It should be about 4 cm wide and its colour must contrast with that of the uniform.

THE GOALKEEPER

A player who is playing in the goalkeeper position may become a court player at any time, following a change of uniform. Similarly, a court player may become a goalkeeper at any time. Goalkeeper substitutions must take place through the substitution area.

The goalkeeper is allowed to:

— touch the ball with any part of his body while in the act of defense inside the goal area;

— move around with the ball inside the goal area without any restriction;

— leave the goal area without the ball and participate in the game in the playing area; when doing so, the goalkeeper becomes subject to the rules applying to players in the playing area;

the goalkeeper is considered to have left the goal area as soon as any part of the body touches the floor outside the goal-area line;

— to leave the goal area together with the ball and play it again in the playing area, if he has not managed to control it fully.

The goalkeeper is not allowed to:

— endanger the opponent while in the act of defense;

— play the ball intentionally out over the outer goal line, after controlling the ball;

— leave the goal area with the ball under control

— touch the ball again outside the goal area following a goalkeeper-throw, unless it has touched another player in between;

— touch the ball when it is stationary or rolling on the floor outside the goal area, while he is inside the goal area;

— take the ball into the goal area when it is stationary or roiling on the floor outside the goal area;

reenter the goal area from the playing area with the ball;

— touch the ball with the foot or the leg below the knee, when it is stationary on the floor in the goal area or moving out towards the playing area;

— cross the goalkeeper's restraining line (4-meter line) or its projection on either side, before the ball has left the thrower's hand when a 7-meter throw is being taken.

THE GOAL AREA

Only the goalkeeper is allowed to enter the goal area. The goal area, which includes the goal-area line, is considered entered when a court player touches it with any part of the body.

When a court player enters the goal area, the decisions shall be as follows;

a) free-throw, when a court player enters the goal area in possession of the ball (1 3:1 c);

b) free-throw, when a court player enters the goal area without the ball but gains an advantage by doing so;

c) 7-meter throw, when a defending player enters the goal area and because of this gains an advantage over an opponent who is in possession of the ball.

A court player entering the goal area is not penalised when:

a) a player enters the goal area after playing the ball, as long as this does not create a disadvantage for the opponents;

b) a player enters the goal area without the ball and does not gain an advantage by doing so;

c) a defending player enters the goal area during or after an attempt to defend, without causing a disadvantage for the opponents;

The ball belongs to the goalkeeper when it is in the goal area. It is not permitted to touch the ball when it is stationary or rolling in the goal area, or when it is held by the goalkeeper. It is permitted, however, to play the ball when it is in the air above the goal area.

The goalkeeper shall put the ball back into play, when it ends up in the goal area. Play shall continue if a player of the defending team touches the ball when in the act defense, and the ball is caught by the goalkeeper or comes to rest in the goal area.

If a player intentionally plays the ball into his own goal area, the decisions shall be as follows:

a) goal, if the ball enters the goal;

b) 7-meter throw, if the goalkeeper touches the ball and it does not enter the goal;

c) free-throw, if the ball comes to a rest in the goal area or goes out over the outer goal line;

d) play continues, if the ball traverses the goal area without being touched be the goalkeeper;

A ball which returns from the goal area out into the playing area remains in play.

PLAYING THE BALL

It is permitted to:

- throw, catch, stop, push or hit the ball, using hands (open or closed), arms, head, torso, thighs and knees;
- hold the ball for a maximum of 3 seconds, even when it is lying on the floor;
- take a maximum of 3 steps with the ball; one step is considered taken when:
  - a) a player who is standing with both feet on the floor lifts one foot and puts it down again, or moves one foot from one place to another;
  - b) a player is touching the floor with one foot only, catches the ball and then touches the floor with the other foot;
  - c) a player after a jump touches the floor with one foot only, and then hops on the same foot or touches the floor with the other foot;
  - d) a player after a jump touches the floor with both feet simultaneously, and then lifts one foot and puts it down again, or moves one foot from one place to another.

While standing or running:

a) bounce the ball once and catch it again with one or both hands;

b) bounce the ball repeatedly with one hand (dribble),

or roll the ball on the floor repeatedly with one hand, and then catch it or pick it up again with one or both hands.

As soon as the ball thereafter is held in one or both hands, it must be played within 3 seconds or after no more than 3 steps. The bouncing or dribbling is considered to have started when the player touches the ball with any part of his body and directs it towards the floor.

After the ball has touched another player or the goal, the player is allowed to tap the ball or bounce it and catch it again.

- move the ball from one hand into the other one.
- to play the ball while kneeling, sitting or laying on the floor.

It is not permitted to:

- touch the ball more than once, unless it has touched the floor, another player, or the goal in the meantime (13:1d).

Fumbling the ball is not penalised.

If the ball has already been controlled, then, the player may not touch it more than once after tapping or bouncing it.

- touch the ball with a foot or leg below the knee, except when the ball has been thrown at the player by an opponent;
- this infraction shall not be penalized, however, if it does not lead to an advantage for the player or his team;

- dive for the ball when it is stationary or rolling on the floor;
- this rule does not apply to the goalkeeper in his own goal area;
- play the ball intentionally out over the side line or the team's own outer goal line; this rule does not apply to the goalkeeper in his own goal area, when he fails to get the ball under control and directs it out over the outer goal line (goalkeeper-throw);
- keep the ball in the team's possession without making any recognisable attempt to attack or to shoot on goal. This is regarded as passive play and is to be penalized with a freethrow for the opponents, from the spot where the ball was when play was interrupted.

Play continues if the ball touches the referee on the court.

THE APPROACH TO THE OPPONENT

It is permitted to:

— use arms and hands to gain possession of the ball;

— use an open hand to play the ball away from the opponent from any direction;

— to obstruct an opponent with the torso, also when the opponent is not in possession of the ball;

It is not permitted to:

- obstruct or restrain an opponent with arms, hands, or legs;
- force an opponent into the goal area;

- pull or hit the ball with one or both hands out of the hand of an opponent; 8:7 use the first to play the ball away from an opponent;
- endanger an opponent with the ball or move the ball towards an opponent in a dangerous fake;
- endanger the goalkeeper;
- reach around or hold an opponent with one or both arms, or to push an opponent;
- run or jump into an opponent, trip an opponent, hit an opponent, or endanger an opponent in any other way.

Infractions of the rules regarding "the Approach to the Opponent" lead to a free-throw" or 7-meter-throw for the opponents..

Infractions of the rules regarding "the Approach to the Opponent" where the action is mainly or exclusively directed at the opponent and not at the ball, are to be punished progressively. Progressive punishment also applies in the case unsportsmanlike conduct. Serious infractions regarding "the Approach to the Opponent" or seriously unsportsmanlike conduct shall be punished through a disqualification of the guilty player. A player who is guilty of assault shall be excluded.

SCORING

- A goal is scored when the entire ball has crossed the entire width of the goal line inside the goal, provided that no infraction of the rules has been committed by the thrower or a teammate before or during the throw.

- A goal shall be allowed, if there is an infection of the rules by a defender but the ball still goes into the goal.
- A goal cannot be awarded, if a referee or the timekeeper has interrupted the game before the ball has completely crossed the goal line.
- A goal shall be awarded to the opponents, if a player plays the ball into his own goal, unless the ball has previously crossed the outer goal line.
- A goal which has been awarded can no longer be disallowed, once the therefore has blown the whistle for the subsequent throw-off to be taken.

The referees must make clear (without a throw-off) that they have allowed a goal, if the signal for the end of a half sounds immediately after a goal is scored and before a throw-off can be taken. The team which has scored more goals than the opponents is the winner. The game is tied if both reams have scored the same number of goals or no goals at all.

THE THROW-OFF

The throw-off is taken by the team which wins the coin toss and elects to start with the ball in possession. The opponents then have the right to choose ends. Alternative, if the team which wins the coin toss prefers to choose ends, then the opponents take the throw-off.

The throw-off at the start of the second half is taken by the team which did not have the throw-off at the start of the game. A new coin toss is undertaken prior to each overtime period. After a goal has been scored, play is resumed by a throw off taken by the team which conceded the goal. The throw-off is taken from the center of the court in any direction. It is preceded by a whistle signal, following which it must be taken within 3 seconds. All players must be in their own half of the court when the throw-off is taken, and the opponents must be at least 3 meters away from the thrower.

THE THROW-IN

A throw-in is awarded when the entire ball has crossed the entire width of the side line, or when a court player on the defending team is the last one to touch the ball before it crosses his team's outer goal line.

The throw-in is taken without whistle signal from the referee, by a player from the opponents of the team whose player last touched the ball before it crossed the line. The throw-in is taken from the spot where the ball crossed the side line or, if it crossed the outer goal line, from the intersection of the side line and the goal line on that side. The thrower must have one toot on the side line until the ball has left his hand.

The player is not allowed to put the ball down on the floor and then pick it up himself, or to bounce the ball and then catch it again himself. While the throw-in is being taken, the opponents may not be closer to the thrower than 3 meters. They are, however, always allowed to stand immediately outside their goalarea line, even if the distance between them and the thrower is then less than 3 meters.

THE GOALKEEPER-THROW

A goalkeeper-throw is awarded when the ball crosses the outer goal line. The goalkeeper-throw is taken without whistle signal from the referee, from the goal area out over the goal-area line. The throw is considered as taken, when the ball thrown by the goalkeeper crosses the goal-area line. If the ball comes to rest in the goal area, the goalkeeper shall put it back into play. The goalkeeper must not touch the ball again after a goalkeeper-throw, until it has touched another player.

THE FREE-THROW

A free-throw is awarded in the event of:

a) faulty substitution or entering the court illegally;

b) infractions by the goalkeeper;

c) infractions by court players in the goal area;

d) infractions when playing the ball

e) intentionally playing the ball across the outer goal line or the side line;

f) passive play;

g) infractions regarding "the Approach to the Opponent";

h) infractions in connection with a throw-off;

i) infractions in connection with a throw-in;

j) infractions in connection with a goalkeeper-throw;

k) infractions in connection with a free-throw;

l) infractions in connection with a 7-meter throw;

m) infractions in connection with a referee-throw;

n) incorrect execution of formal throws;

o) unsportsmanlike conduct;

p) assault.

The free-throw is taken without any whistle signal from the referee and, in principle, from the place where the infraction occurred.

If this place is located between the goal-area line and the 9-meter line of the team committing the infraction, then the free-throw shall be taken from the nearest point immediately outside the 9-meter line. Once an attacker is in the correct position for the throw, with the ball in hand, he must not put it down on the floor and pick it up again, or bounce it and catch it again. Players of the attacking team must not touch or cross the 9-meter line of the opponents before the freethrow has been taken.

The referees must correct the positions of attacking players who are between the 9-meter line and the goal-area line during the execution of the free-throw, if the incorrect positions have an influence on the game. The free-throw shall then be taken following a whistle signal.

When a freethrow is being taken, the opponents must remain at a distance of at least 3 meters from the thrower. They are, however, allowed to stand immediately outside their goal-area line, even if the free-throw is being taken from their 9-meter line. The referees must refrain from awarding a free-throw for an infraction on the part of the defending team, if this would lead to a disadvantage for the attacking team.

At least a free-throw must be awarded if an infraction causes the attacking team to lose possession of the ball. A free-throw must not be awarded, if the player retains full control of ball and body despite the infraction.

If a game is interrupted although there is no infraction of the rules, then a team which is in possession of the ball shall retain possession. The game is restarted with a free-throw for that team, from the place where the ball was at the time of the interruption. The free-throw must be preceded by a whistle signal. If there is a decision against the attacking team, and a player from that team is in possession of the ball at the time, then he must put it down on the floor immediately.

The 7-Meter Throw

A 7-meter throw is awarded when:

a) a clear chance of scoring is destroyed anywhere on the court, also if it is done by a team official;

b) a goalkeeper enters his goal area with the ball, or takes it into the goal area when he is inside;

c) a court player intentionally plays the ball to his own goalkeeper in the goal area and the goalkeeper touches the ball;

d) a court player intentionally plays the ball to his own goalkeeper in the goal area and the goalkeeper touches the ball;

e) there is an unwarranted whistle signal at the time of a clear chance of scoring;

f) a clear chance of scoring is destroyed through the interference of someone not authorised to be on the court.

The 7-meter throw is to be taken as a shot n goal, within 3 seconds after a whistle signal from the court referee. The player who is taking the 7-meter throw must not touch or cross the 7-meter line before the ball has left his hand. The ball must not be played again following the execution of a 7-meter throw, until it has touched the goalkeeper or the goal. No player other than the thrower is allowed to be in the area between the 9-meter line and the goal-area line while a 7-meter throw is being taken.

A free-throw shall be awarded to the defending team, if a player of the attacking team touches or crosses the 9-meter line before the ball has left the thrower" hand. The players of the defending team must be at least 3 meters from the 7-meter line while a 7-meter throw is being taken. If a defending player touches or crosses the 9-meter line or moves closer than 3 meters from the 7-meter line before the ball has left the thrower's- hand, the decisions shall be as follows:

a) goal, if the ball goes into the goal;

b) retaking of the 7-meter throw in all other cases.

The 7-meter throw is to be retaken, unless a goal was scored, if a goalkeeper crosses his restraining line i.e., the 4-meter line, before the ball leaves the thrower's hand. The referees must refrain from awarding a 7-meter throw for an infraction by the defending team, if this would lead to a disadvantage for the attacking team.

At least a 7-meter throw must be awarded, if a clear chance of scoring is destroyed and no goal results, because of an infraction, an act of unsportsmanlike conduct, an unwarranted Whistle signal, or the interference by someone who is not part of the game.

A 7-meter throw must not be awarded if the attacking players retains full ball and body control despite the infraction.

The Referee-Throw

The game is restarted with a referee-throw if:

a) there are simultaneous infractions on the court by players from both teams;

b) the ball touches the ceiling or any fixture above the court;

c) the game was interrupted although there was no infraction, and neither team was in possession of the ball.

There shall always be a "Time-out" when a referee-throw is called). The referee-throw is taken at the center of the court. The court referee throws the ball vertically following a whistle signal.

With the exception of one player from each team, all players must remain at least 3 meters away from the referee while the referee-throw is being taken. The two players who are jumping for the ball shall stand next to the referee, each on the side nearest to his own goal. The ball may be played only after it has reached its highest point.

THE EXECUTION OF THE FORMAL THROWS

All players must be in the positions prescribed for the throw in question. An incorrect initial position is to be corrected. The ball must be in the hand of the thrower before a throw is executed. When a throw-off, throw-in, free-throw, or 7-meter throw is taken, the thrower must have one part of a toot in constant contact with the floor.

The other foot may be lifted and put down repeatedly. The referee must blow the whistle for the restart:

a. when the game is restarted in certain situations;

b. when the execution of a throw-in, goalkeeper-throw, or free-throw has been delayed;

c. after a correction or caution;

d. after a warning

e. after a 2-minute suspension is given;

f. after a disqualification

g. after an exclusion

h. when the referees have indicated different opinions as to which team should be penalised.

After the whistle signal, the thrower must play the ball within 3 seconds. A throw is considered taken when the ball has left the hand of the thrower. The ball may not be handed over to, or touched by, a teammate of the thrower when the throw is being taken.

The thrower must not touch the ball again until it has touched another player or the goal. A goal may be scored directly from any throw.

Incorrect positions on the part of the defending players in connection with the execution of throw-in or a free-throw must not be corrected by the referees, if the attacking players are not at a disadvantage by taking the throw immediately. If there is a disadvantage, then the positions are to be corrected. If the referee blows his whistle for a throw to be taken, despite incorrect positions on the part of defending players, then those players are fully entitled to interfere. A player is to be warned if he delays or interferes with the execution of a throw by the opponents, by standing too close or through other infractions. He is to be suspended if he repeats it.

THE PUNISHMENTS

A warning can be given for:

a) infractions concerning "the Approach to the Opponent".

A warning shall be given for:

b) such infractions concerning "the Approach to the Opponent" which are to be punished progressively;

c) infractions when the opponents are executing a formal throw;

d) unsportsmanlike conduct by a player or team official.

The referee shall indicate the warning to the guilty player or official and to the timekeeper/scorekeeper by holding up a yellow card.

An individual player should not be given more than one warning, and a team should not be given more than 3 warnings. A player who has already had a 2-minutes suspension should not subsequently be given a warning. No more than one warning should be given to the officials of a team.

A suspension (2 minutes) shall be given:

a) for a faulty substitution or illegal entering of the court;

b) for repeated infractions concerning "the Approach-to the Opponent" which are of the type that they are to be punished progressively;

c) for repeated unsportsmanlike conduct by a player on the court;

d) for failure to put the ball down on the floor when a decision is taken against the attacking team;

e) for repeated infractions when the opponents are executing a formal throw;

f) as a consequence of a disqualification of a player or team official.

In exceptional circumstances, a suspension can be given without a prior warning. The referee shall clearly indicate the suspension to the guilty player and to the timekeeper/scorekeeper through the prescribed hand signal, i.e., one arm raised with two fingers extended. The suspension is always for a playing time of 2 minutes; the third suspension for the same player always leads to a disqualification. The suspended player is not allowed to participate in the game during his suspension time, and the team is not allowed to replace him on the court.

The suspension period begins when play is restarted with a whistle signal. A 2-minute suspension carries over to the second half of the game if it has not been completed by the end of the first half. The same applies from regulation time to overtime and during overtime.

A disqualification shall be given:

a) if a player who is not entitled to participate enters the court;

b) for serious infractions concerning "the Approach to the opponent";

c) for repeated unsportsmanlike conduct by a team official, or by a player who is outside the court;

d) for seriously unsportsmanlike conduct by a player or a team official;

e) because of a third suspension to the same player;

f) for an assault by a team official..

The disqualification of a player or a team official during the playing time always leads to a 2-minute suspension, i.e., the team's strength on the court is reduced by one. The referee shall indicate the disqualification to the guilty player or official and to the timekeeper/scorekeeper by holding up a red card. A disqualification of a player or team official always applies for the remaining playing time. The player or official must leave the court and the substitution area immediately. A disqualification reduces the number of players, or officials, that is available to the team. The team is, however, allowed to increase the number of players on the court following the expiration of the 2-minute suspension.

An exclusion shall be given in the event of an assault during the playing time, also outside the playing court.

The referees shall call a "time-out" and inform the guilty player and the timekeeper/scorekeeper directly. The prescribed hand signal to be used by the referee in front of the player is to cross the arms in face height. An exclusion always applies to the remaining playing time, and the team must continue with one player less on the court. The excluded player must not be replaced and must leave both the court and the substitution area immediately.

If a player who has just been given a 2-minute suspension is guilty of another infraction before the game is restarted, then only the most severe one of the applicable punishments shall be given. If a goalkeeper is suspended, disqualified, or excluded, another player must take up the goalkeeper position.

The referees have to warn a player whom they find guilty of unsportsmanlike conduct, irrespective of whether this takes place on or outside the court. If the conduct is repeated, then a player who is on the court shall be suspended, whereas a player who is outside the court (a substitute or a suspended player) shall be disqualified.

A team official who is guilty of unsportsmanlike conduct shall be given a warning. He shall be disqualified if the conduct is repeated. If unsportsmanlike conduct or an assault takes place when the game is already interrupted, then the game shall be restarted in a manner which corresponds to the reason for that interruption.

Unsportsmanlike conduct or an assault taking place on the premises where a game is played, shall be punished as follows:

Before the game:

a) a warning shall the given in the case of unsportsmanlike conduct;

b) a disqualification shall be given in the case of seriously unsportsmanlike conduct or assault, but the team is allowed to start with 12 players:

During an intermission:

c) a warning shall be given in the case of unsportsmanlike conduct;

d) a disqualification shall be given in the case of repeated or seriously unsportsmanlike conduct or in the case of an assault;

After the game:

e) a written report.

THE REFEREES

- Two referees with equal authority shall be in charge of each game. They are assisted by a timekeeper and a scorekeeper.
- The referees monitor the conduct of the players from the moment they enter the premises until they leave.
- The referees are responsible for inspecting the playing court, the goals, and the balls before the game starts (3:1); they decide which ball will be used. The referee who is officially listed first shall decide if they have different opinions.
- The referees also establish the presence of both teams in proper uniforms. They check the scoresheet and the equipment of the players. They ensure that the number of players and officials in the substitution area is within the limits, and they establish the presence and identity of the "responsible team official" for each team.

  Any discrepancies must be corrected.

The coin toss is undertaken by the referee who is officially listed first, in the presence of the other referee and both team captains. At the start of the game, the referee listed second takes up the position as court referee behind the team which is taking the throw-off. The court referee starts the game with a whistle signal for the throw-off. When subsequently the other team gains possession of the ball, the referee listed second takes up the position on the goal-line of the now defending team. The other referee starts as goal-line referee at the other goal line. He becomes court referee, when the team at that end gains possession.

The referees must change ends with each other from time to time during the game. In principle, the entire game shall be conducted by the same two referees. It is their responsibility to ensure that the game is played in accordance with the rules, and they must penalize any infractions. If one of the referees becomes unable to finish the game, the other referee will continue the game alone.

In principle, the court referee whistles for:

a) the execution of all formal throws in accordance with rules, and after time-out;

b) the expiration of the playing time, if the automatic signal has not sounded or the timekeeper has not given the final signal.

In principle, the goal-line referee whistle:

c) When a goal has been scored.

If both referees whistle for an infraction and agree as to which team should be penalised but have different opinion as to the severity of the punishment, then the most severe of the two punishments should be given. If both referees whistle for an infraction but have different opinions as to which team should be penalized, then the opinion of the court referee always prevails.

The game is restarted following clear hand signals from the court referee and a whistle signal. Both referees are responsible for keeping the score. They also take notes about warnings, suspension, disqualifications, and exclusions.

Both referees are responsible for controlling the playing time. If there is any doubt about the accuracy of the timekeeping, the referee who is officially listed first will decide. The referees are responsible for ensuring after the game that the scoresheet is completed correctly. Decisions made by the referees on the basis of their observations of facts are final.

Appeals can be lodged against decisions which are not in conformity with the rules. During the game, the team captains are entitled to address the referees.

Both referees have the right to suspend a game temporarily or permanently. Every effort must be made to continue the game, before a decision is taken to suspend it permanently. The black uniform is reserved for the referees.

THE SCOREKEEPER AND THE TIMEKEEPER

The scorekeeper checks the team rosters; only the players listed are entitled to participate. The scorekeeper, together with the timekeeper, checks the entering of players who have arrived after the game started or are reentering after a suspension. The scorekeeper is in charge of the scoresheet and makes the necessary notations (goals, warnings, suspensions, disqualifications, and exclusions).

The timekeeper controls:

a) the playing time; the referees decide when the clock is to be stopped and restarted;

b) the number of players and officials in the substitution area;

c) together with the scorekeeper, the entering of players who have arrived after the game started;

d) the exit and entry of the substituting players

e) the entering of players who are not entitled to participate;

f) the suspension time of suspended players;

It is the task of the timekeeper to give a loud signal to stop the game at the end of a half, if there is no public clock with automatic final signal available.

When there has been an interruption of the playing time (time-out), the timekeeper must inform the responsible team official for each team about how much time has been played or how much time is left (except when there is a public clock). The timekeeper informs the suspended player or the responsible team official when the suspension time expires.

The Standard IHF hand signals

When infractions are called, the referees must show immediately the direction for the throw which is to follow. Only when there could be some doubt about the reason for the call, shall the referee give the relevant hand signal (except in the case of signals 11- 1 8 which are mandatory).

The list of the hand signals:

1 Entering the goal area

2 Illegal dribble

3 Too many steps, or holding the ball more than 3 seconds

4 Reaching around, holding, or pushing

5 Hitting

6 Attacker's fault- running into, jumping into

7 Throw-in

8 Goalkeeper-throw

9 Free-throw-direction

10 Keep the distance of 3 meters

11 Passive play

12 Goal

13 Referee-throw

14 Warning (yellow); Disqualification (red)

15 Suspension (2 minutes)

16 Exclusion

17 Time-out

18 Permission to enter the court during time-out

Infractions during a time-out have the same consequences as infractions during the playing time.

When is playing time to be interrupted?

Obligatory:

a) when a disqualification or exclusion is given

b) when a referee-throw is called

In principle, in the event of:

c) extraordinary incidents (e.g., spectators or objects on the court, damage to a goal or the ball, the ball is lost in/under the stands, water/condensation on the court, power failure);

d) necessary consultations between the referees or with the timekeeper/scorekeeper;

e) suspected injuries (e.g., the ball hits a player in the head)

f) a signal from the timekeeper/scorekeeper;

As the occasion demands, in the event of:

g) a delay in the execution of a formal throw;

h) a warning or suspension;

i) a goalkeeper substitution at the time of a 7-meter throw;

j) a faulty substitution or when an extra player enters the court;

k) a player throwing the ball away or not giving it up.

Goalkeeper substitution at the time of a 7-meter throw

It is no longer permitted to change goalkeepers once the thrower is ready to take the 7-meter throw, standing in the correct position with the ball in hand. (The goalkeeper shall be given a warning for unsportsmanlike conduct in accordance with 17:Id, if he still tries to leave the goal in this situation, and he must remain in goal); He shall be given a 2-minute suspension if he still goes through with the substitution; He is also to be suspended, when initially trying to leave his goal, if he already has a warning or if his team already has a total of three warnings; It does not make any difference whether or not the initiative to the substitution comes from a team official.

Several infractions in connection with a substitution

If several players each commit an infraction in connection with a substitution, only the first player committing an infraction is to be penalised.

Headbands are allowed for the purpose of confining long hair, as long as they are made of a soft, elastic material.

Entering the goal area during a clear chance of scoring

Situation: an attacking player is waiting for the ball immediately outside the goal-area line, when the ball is rebounding from the goal or the goalkeeper; the defending court player has no chance of getting the ball without committing an infraction; to prevent a clear chance of scoring from arising, the defender enters the goal area and prevents the attacker from catching the ball.

If the referees are convinced that, in these particular circumstances, a clear chance of scoring was taken away, they must award a 7-meter throw.

Progressive punishment

Progressive punishment means that it is not sufficient to penalize a particular foul against an opponent with a free-throw only, because the foul goes beyond the type of infraction which may normally occur in the struggle for the ball. "Actions" directed mainly or exclusively at the opponent and not the ball are to be punished progressively. Basically this includes infractions directed at the body of the opponent, such as reaching around, holding, pushing, running or jumping into, tripping, or hitting the opponent. Obstruction, although directed at the body of the opponent, is obviously allowed.

Each infraction which meets the definition for progressive punishment is to be punished, beginning with a warning, and with a trend of increasingly severe punishments. Warnings and suspension which are given for other reasons (e.g., standing too close, or not giving up the ball), are to be taken into account in the progressivity, just like the punishments for unsportsmanlike conduct.

Unsportsmanlike conduct

Examples of unsportsmanlike conduct are:

a) shouting at the player who is taking a 7-meter throw;

b) kicking the ball away during a stoppage, so that the opponent cannot immediately execute the throw that has been awarded;

c) verbally abusing an opponent or a teammate;

d) when a substitute or team official does not give up the ball when it has ended up outside the side line;

e) delaying the execution of a formal throw;

f) grabbing the uniform of an opponent;

g) if a goalkeeper has requested permission for substitution at a 7-meter throw, thus causing the referees to give "time-out" and then returns to the goal after going out to the substitution area;

h) if a goalkeeper does not give up the ball when a 7-meter throw has been awarded to the opponent;

i) repeatedly blocking shots with the foot or the lower leg.

Examples of serious infractions are:

a) pulling back the arm of a shooting opponent, without any recognisable intention to reach the ball;

b) holding or pulling down an opponent who is running in a counterattack;

c) pushing an opponent who is taking a jump shot, without any recognizable intention to reach to the ball;

d) clearly deliberate tripping;

e) hitting the goalkeeper in the head with a 7-meter throw, if the goalkeeper is not moving.

Seriously unsportsmanlike conduct

Examples of seriously unsportsmanlike conduct are:

a) offences against a referee;

b) throwing or pushing the ball away after a decision by the referees, if the ball goes so far that it cannot be seen as just unsportsmanlike conduct;

c) if the goalkeeper demonstrates such a passive attitude when a 7-meter throw has been awarded to the opponent, that the referee must assume that he is not trying to stop the shot;

d) taking revenge after having been fouled (hitting back in a reflex action);

e) deliberately throwing the ball at an opponent during a stoppage in the game, unless it is done in such a way that it must be regarded as an assault.

Location for the execution of a free-throw

In principle, the free-throw shall be taken from the location where the infraction was committed. A player who infringes Rule (i.e., not putting the ball down when a call has been made in favour of the opponents) shall be given a 2-minute suspension, and the free-throw shall be taken from the place where the infraction that led to the call was committed.

In other situations, it is permitted to execute the free-throw from the place where the ball is, provided that the distance between this place and the place of the infraction is within the acceptable margin. This margin is about 3 meters at the executing team's own goal-area line and then gradually narrows down to zero for a free-throw taken from the 9-meter line of the opponents.

Consequences of a direct disqualification

A disqualification because of a serious infraction or seriously unsportsmanlike conduct applies, in principle, only to the remainder of the game in which it is given. It is to be regarded as decision by the referees on the basis of their observations of facts. Except in cases involving offenses against the referees, there shall be no further consequences of the disqualification beyond the game.

A disqualification of a team official, a player in the substitution area, or a player serving a 2-minute suspension, always leads to a deduction of the team on the court for 2 minutes. This, "another player" must leave the court for these 2 minutes. If a player who has just been suspended commits another infraction before the game is restarted, this is to be regarded as one continued infraction and only one punishment, the most severe one applicable to any of the actions, shall be given.

If the further infraction takes place only after the game has been restarted, then the player is disqualified. The guilty player also receives a further 2-minute suspension, which must be served by "another player".

INTERRUPTION OF THE GAME

If the game has been interrupted by the referees because a player or team official is to be cautioned or penalized, then the game must be restarted with a free-throw for the opponents from the place of the infraction. Alteratively, a 7-meter throw is to be awarded if there was a clear chance of scoring when the game was interrupted. If the game has been interrupted by the timekeeper or scorekeeper, then the game shall be resumed with the throw that corresponds to the game situation at the time of the interruption.

Substitution area regulations

The substitution areas are situated to the left and right of a continuation of the center, line, up to 1.5 m outside the side line and also behind the team benches if space allows.

Nothing of any description whatsoever may be allowed to stand near the side lines throughout the outer end of the substitution benches (at least 8 m from the center line). Only the players and team officials entered on the scoresheet may be allowed to stay in the substitution area.

If an interpreter is necessary, he must take up his position behind the team bench. Players and team officials who wish to leave the substitution area, must inform the timekeeper/scorekeeper, through the responsible team official, when they leave and when they return.

The team officials in the substitution area must be fully dressed in sports wear or civilian clothing. The timekeeper-scorekeeper shall support the referees in monitoring the occupancy of the substitution area before and during the game.

If before the game there are any infringements of the rules as regards the substitution areas, the game may not start until they have been straightened out. If such rules are infringed during a game, the game may not be, continued after the next interruption until they have corrected.

The team officials have the right and duty to guide and manage their team during the game, in a fair and sporting spirit within the framework of the rules. The team officials and players who are in the substitution area shall basically sit on the team bench.

It is, however, permitted to stand up only briefly:

a) when players are substituted;

b) to give advice on tactics to players on the court and on the bench;

c) to give medical care;

d) to warm up, without a ball, behind the team bench, if there is sufficient room and if it is not disturbing;

e) to communicate with the timekeeper/scorekeeper (this only applies to the responsible team official and only in exceptional circumstances.

It is not permitted:

a) to stand or walk in front of, behind, or next to the team bench for more than a brief moment in a manner which is disturbing;

b) for players or team officials to interfere with or insult referees, timekeeper/scorekeeper, other players or team officials, or spectators by behaving in a provoking, protesting, or otherwise unsportsmanlike manner (speech, mimic, or gestures);

c) to leave the substitution area in order to influence the game;

d) to stand or move on the side line while warming up.

If the substitution area regulations are infringed, the referees are obliged to act in accordance with rules (warning, disqualification). If the referees fail to notice an infringement of the substitution area regulations, they must be informed about it be the timekeeper/scorekeeper during the next interruption of the game.

An IHF representative or an official representative of the organizing federation who is on duty at a game is allowed to interrupt the game and draw the attention of the referees to a possible violation of the rules, except in the case of decisions made by the referees on the basis of their observations of facts.

If the referees do not take action against an infringement of the substitution area regulations, even if they have been made aware of it, then the IHF representative (or official federation representative) must submit a report to the appropriate authority (e.g., disciplinary committee). This authority decides about the events in the substitution area and about the attitude of the referees.

INDEX